FREE
LOOKS GOOD ON
YOU

*Healing the
Soul Wounds of
Toxic Love*

CHRISTY JOHNSON

Free Looks Good on You
Copyright 2020 by Christy Johnson
Christy Johnson

Cover design by Ryan Lause
Edited by Robin Patchen

Unless otherwise specified, Scripture quotations are taken from *The Holy Bible, New International Version®* NIV®. Copyright © 1973, 1978, 1984, 2011 by Biblica, Inc.™ Used by permission of Zondervan. All rights reserved worldwide. www.zondervan.com. The "NIV" and "New International Version" are trademarks registered in the United States Patent and Trademark Office by Biblica, Inc.™

Other versions used are:

KJV—*King James Version,* Authorized King James Version.

NASB—Scripture taken from the *New American Standard Bible®,* Copyright © 1960, 1962, 1963, 1968, 1971, 1972, 1973, 1975, 1977, 1995 by The Lockman Foundation. Used by permission. (www.Lockman.org).

NKJV—Scripture taken from the *New King James Version.* Copyright © 1982 by Thomas Nelson, Inc. Used by permission. All rights reserved.

NLT—Scripture quotations marked (NLT) are taken from the *Holy Bible, New Living Translation,* copyright © 1996, 2004, 2007 by Tyndale House Foundation. Used by permission of Tyndale House Publishers, Inc., Carol Stream, Illinois 60188. All rights reserved.

The Message—Scripture taken from The Message. Copyright Â© 1993, 1994, 1995, 1996, 2000, 2001, 2002. Used by permission of NavPress Publishing Group.

Published by Christy Johnson
Edmond, OK 73013

Library of Congress Cataloging-in-Publication Data

Johnson, Christy

    Free Looks Good on You: Healing the Soul Wounds of Toxic Love / Christy Johnson
p. cm.

ISBN 978-1-7320193-1-7 (paperback)
    978-1-7320193-2-4 (e-book)
    978-1-7320193-3-1 (audio book)

Printed in the United States of America

All rights reserved. No part of this book may be reproduced or transmitted in any form or by any means, electronic or mechanical, including photocopying and recording, or by any information storage and retrieval system, without permission in writing from the publisher.

WHAT OTHERS ARE SAYING ABOUT FREE LOOKS GOOD ON YOU

"If you ever thought you'd never get over him and what he's done, this book will change all that. With clear action points and biblical strategies, you'll learn how to remove the sting of the past and fall in love with life again."
—**Shannon Ethridge, M.A.**, Life/Relationship Coach & Author of 22 books including the million-copy best-selling Every Woman's Battle series and *The Sexually Confident Wife*

"Christy Johnson's authenticity and transparent story telling is refreshing. Reading *Free Looks Good on You* is like sitting down and talking with a close friend...the kind that doesn't judge you but actually gives useful advice and solid wisdom."
—**Robia Scott**, Author of *Counterfeit Comforts* and Actress in *Unplanned*

"Riveting. Christy has lived through betrayal, abuse and addiction, but with life-changing truth, never has the subject of recovering from romantic soul wounds been covered with such powerful grace. When you finish this book, you'll know without a doubt that if Christy can be free—so can you."
—**Melanie Hemry**, Author, ghostwriter and two-time winner of the Angel Award, the most prestigious writing award in Christian publishing.

Dedication

I dedicate this book to Jacob Isaiah Ennis, my youngest son. Jake, I know you're in heaven standing with the cloud of witnesses cheering me on. Your life truly lives on in me.

Foreword

I FIRST MET CHRISTY at a professional conference we both attended. She was hard to miss. Tall, blonde, and gorgeous. Yet I also saw an inner strength radiating from her that made me curious about who she was beneath her outer beauty and where that depth of strength came from.

Fast forward a few years later and Christy invited me to preview her new book, *Free Looks Good on You*. I loved the title. What woman doesn't want to look good? We can spend hours paying attention to our outer beauty, but often neglect our inner work.

I was anxious to read what Christy had to say to a woman who doesn't feel free. Who feels damaged, ugly, broken, discarded, abandoned, or in bondage to her own anger, depression, and resentment. What wisdom would she offer a woman enslaved by the fear of man, terrified of rejection or trapped in lies she's believed or has been told about her worth? I wanted to know more about her own story, her own journey, and exactly how she became free.

All I can say is wow, wow, wow. Looking at her now, I would have never guessed her pain and heartache married to an addicted and abusive man. Of tragically losing her little boy because of her husband's recklessness. Of sinking into despair and battling resentment and rage over what happened to her. Christy is a woman who can show other women the way to freedom because she has done her own work when it would have been far easier for her to stay angry, depressed, bitter and despairing.

Indeed, free looks good on her. And, as a Christian counselor and coach for over 40 years, I've worked with thousands of women who have been deeply wounded by others. Childhood sexual, physical and emotional abuse, marital rape and abuse, deceit, sexual addictions, verbal abuse, spiritual oppression and manipulation have left their scars deeply etched on a woman's soul and spirit. Yes, therapy, support, and coaching can help a woman heal, but only God can set her free. Free from her rightful anger over what's happened to her. Free from her resentment and bitterness. Free from the lies she's believed. Sadly, I've seen too many women stay stuck, trapped in feeling powerless and hopeless, scared and depleted. Living in bondage and fear, not freedom.

Christy's book, *Free Looks Good on You* gives a woman a clear and doable blueprint toward freedom. It is sound theologically and highly practical. Even as a committed Christian, a wounded woman struggles with how to forgive the unforgivable. She knows she should. She knows God commands it. But how do you do it? How do you let go of your rage when everything feels so terribly unjust and unfair? Why does the bad guy get away with it and the good one's suffer? She wonders if she will ever find peace. Will she ever feel joyful or happy or simply safe again?

God has hardwired our human brain for two main functions. One is to protect ourselves from harm and the other is to grow and flourish. When a woman is harmed or threatened her brain and body reacts like God designed. It moves into protection and survival mode. Growth always takes a back seat until she can be and feel safe. She might need physical safety but often even after she is physically safe, her brain/body continues to feel emotionally, mentally and relationally terrified.

In her humanness and sinfulness, she often develops unhealthy coping mechanisms to calm herself down or feel better. She may use denial so she doesn't have to face the truth of what happened or the danger she is still in. She may use rage to protect herself against further harm. Or, she may turn to food, alcohol, drugs or sex to numb herself.

When fear is in charge, there is no energy for growth. Instead all of a woman's energy gets used to self-protect. Even after the crisis is long over, fear remains. Instead of growth, she survives by numbing herself, avoiding her problems, and blaming others, God, or life for how unfair and miserable her life has turned out. But this doesn't have to be the end of her story or yours.

Christy never minimizes her struggle or the daily battle she faced. She vulnerably shares her own unhealthy self-protective coping strategies and gives you specific action plans so that you too can turn the corner and learn, step by step to live free. In each chapter she wants you to ponder what you're learning and practice new ways of thinking, talking, praying, and living.

In her book, Christy uses the metaphor of a castle to help you picture what safety and freedom look like. She teaches you how to be a detective, investigating your own life patterns in order to gain greater self-awareness. She wants you to discover the beliefs you have that keep you stuck and helpless. Belief's like "I have to be perfect in order to be okay." Or "I shouldn't trust my own instincts." Or "I'm not worth anything."

Christy also helps you uncover the deeper stories you tell yourself that actually limit your choices and your freedom. Her powerful chapter on how words create our reality will unlock the prison door for you and open up new choices that you never thought possible.

The woman of Proverbs 31 is described as a woman of strength and dignity, who smiles at the future unafraid. That is God's desire for you. Christy's book gives you the blueprint and teaches you how to hold your Father's hand out of bondage and into freedom.

Leslie Vernick MSW
Relationship coach, speaker, author of the best-selling books, *The Emotionally Destructive Marriage* and *The Emotionally Destructive Relationship*

Acknowledgments

JOHN, MY HEAVEN-SENT HUSBAND, I've said it before, but I have to say it again. I couldn't do what I do without your support and encouragement. You've never complained about the hours I spend writing and planning and coaching. Your prayers before every event and every coaching session prove your dedication to see women find their freedom in Christ. Your name's not on this book, but you are the man behind the scenes that makes my purpose possible.

To my son Garrett, thank you for producing the audio version of this book and listening to countless hours of your mom narrating every word. I'll never forget the moments we shared as I read various scenes from the past. At random times, my throat grew so tight with emotion, no words would form. Then I'd look at you. Sitting at your mobile recording studio with your headphones on, you were trying so hard to be quiet so you didn't mess up the recording, but your face held rivers of tears.

I may never get to witness anyone else hearing my entire manuscript, but I'm so glad I got to share it with you. You did so much more than record an audio book. You were not only an eye witness to much of what I've written, but when you listened to me read, your tears endorsed the message of this book. Your tender heart means the world to me.

My daughters, Brittany and Melissa. You are my greatest cheerleaders, abounding in encouragement. Your never-ending spirit of positivity and you-can-do-this attitude has kept me going many times when doubts collided with my vision.

Cheri Fuller, Rene Gutteridge, Christopher Maselli, Laurel Thomas and Melanie Hemry, the joy of serving with you on the Write Well, Sell Well team over the past several years has been one of the greatest privileges of my writing career. I've learned from the best— Cheri Fuller, the magazine master, Rene the effortless comic and screenwriter, Chris the marketing guru, Laurel the queen of scene description and Melanie, a magician with words. I'll never forget the first time I was invited to one of your workshops. I knew I stood in the midst of a legend. I devoured every article you wrote for the *Believers Voice of Victory*. And now to think I'm in your critique group. Your teaching helped me win the Guideposts Writers Workshop in 2018 and helped me polish every paragraph in this book. I'm overjoyed to follow in your footsteps.

To the girls in my Mastermind Group—Erin Taylor Young, Robin Patchen, Misty Beller and Laura McClellan, thank you so much for the invitation to join! The wisdom I've gained over the past few years from each of you is priceless, but your prayers and fellowship are the reason for my growth. I count myself blessed to be in your league!

To Robin Patchen, my editor. You caught every unfinished thought, every vague description and every unanswered question. I'm glad you didn't let me off easy. Your editorial genius and devotion to truth made this a much better book!

And finally, to my readers and coaching clients. When my life was full of bitterness and regret, faithful women stood by me and helped me climb out of my pit of despair. Now I consider it a great joy and an honor to pass on the blessing. What a thrill it is to see you discard old mindsets and lies from the enemy and begin to flourish in God's truth for your life. This book is for you!

Here's to your freedom!

Table of Contents

Part I
How Did We Get This Way?

1. When the Pain Won't Stop 15
2. What's Poisoning My Soul? 26
3. Roots of Resentment 39
4. Counterfeit Comforters 51
5. Father Wounds 68
6. Defeating a Victim Mentality 82

Part II
The Freedom Blueprint 100

7. Looking Back to Look Out 107
8. Self-Talk Matters 125
9. Changing My Vision 142
10. Rewriting My Life Script 163
11. Setting Boundaries That Stick 187
12. Spot and Stop Manipulation 201
13. Where is the Holy Spirit in All of This Chaos? ... 215
14. The Leverage of Forgiveness 231
15. The View From the Watchtower 249
16. Divine Whispers 264
17. Safe in the Keep 277
18. Free at Last 293

Notes 307

- 1 -

WHEN THE PAIN WON'T STOP

June 12, 1998

THE LINGERING RAYS OF THE afternoon sun shone through my kitchen window accentuating the cobalt blue mosaic tile on the backsplash as I washed Jacob's sippy cup. I listened as my two sons, five-year-old Garrett and two-year-old Jacob played in the backyard under the limbs of our pecan trees. Their laughter sent tsunami waves of joy through me. Music from twelve-year-old Brittany's room blared through the house. Pulling my hands from the soapy water, I leaned against the counter, weak with gratitude.

Normal, everyday sounds of a happy family were proof that we'd moved on after the divorce. I no longer had to worry about being threatened with a shotgun or that my kids would find drugs lying around the house after their father shot up or popped a handful of pills. No more abuse and addiction. No more drug-induced manic episodes. No more lying, manipulation and deceit.

We were safe in our new home, making a new start.

I looked around the house my father had helped me buy out of foreclosure. Although small, it was a gingerbread cottage straight out of a fairy tale. It had needed a lot of love, but I'd had plenty to give. A charming cobblestone path wound its way to the original front door from 1948. Underneath old carpet, I'd found hardwood floors, which now gleamed. The house had lots of historical charm with glossy white trim and plenty of built-ins. I loved sipping tea in my Adirondack chair and watching the kids play in the yard. After ten years of living with control, chaos and confusion, I had security at last. My fresh start. My new life.

Moments like this still hit me on a regular basis. The sense of overwhelming gratitude that my kids and I were safe. My ex-husband, Tom, now lived with his parents who provided a safe place for my children to visit their father. They watched over Tom, trying to keep him in line and making sure he didn't drive unless he was sober. I knew they would lay down their lives for my kids.

The kids loved going to Nanny and Papa's house. His parents had also been granted custody of his sister's three children. Nanny and Papa spoiled them all with late nights and no rules. Despite the obvious chaos of six kids and three adults crammed into a two-bedroom home, to the kids, it was an extended slumber party of sheer delight. Great fried food, no set bedtime, and at least one fight with a cousin—the ultimate definition of fun.

"Mommy!" Brittany stepped into the kitchen. "Natasha invited me to spend the weekend with her at her grandmother's lake house!" Brittany's blonde locks danced on her shoulders as she bounced up and down. "Can I go? Please?"

"I'm sorry, baby, I can't let you go. It's your dad's weekend and he'll be here any minute."

"Just this once? I really want to go!"

"I know, honey, but there'll be another time."

Brittany was very compliant for a twelve-year-old, but now she acted like an attorney pleading a case. She refused to give it a rest.

Later, I looked at the clock and realized that Tom was an hour late. Typical. I knew better than to expect a courtesy call. "All right. You can go."

Grabbing her reprieve like a lifeline, Brittany called Natasha and was gone before I had time for more than a quick hug and kiss. She was smart to get out before her dad arrived.

"Come on boys," I called a while later. "Daddy's here."

Squeals of delight echoed through the house followed by the pitter-patter of little feet racing out the door to see Daddy.

"Have a good time at Nanny's," I said as I kissed Garrett goodbye.

"I will, Mommy," said Garrett.

"I'm going to miss you, baby." I started to buckle Jake's seatbelt. His pudgy hands pushed mine away.

"I do it, Mommy," he insisted. "I big boy!"

"You sure are." I clicked the seatbelt into place, letting him help. "Give Mommy a kiss."

As the truck drove away, the boys and I waved and blew kisses until they were out of sight.

It was Friday evening, the weekend of my Twentieth High School Reunion. I didn't know what to expect. I hadn't seen most of these people since the ten-year reunion, but Friday evening turned out great. I spent the evening catching up with old friends, and, even though my fiancé, John, didn't know anyone, he had no trouble mixing with the crowd. The next day promised to be even more fun. A picnic was scheduled for Saturday morning at ten-thirty, and the reunion culminated with a semi-formal dinner that evening.

Saturday morning when the doorbell rang, I glanced at the clock and realized it was already ten. I always was rushing around at the last minute, and John was always early. My sandals slapped the hardwood floor as I ran to answer the door.

John came in for a moment while I finished gathering my things for the picnic. As I grabbed my purse to leave, my feet planted a firm stop just before the door.

"Wait just a sec," I said whirling around. "I've gotta show you something before we leave."

I grabbed a stack of photos off the coffee table. "I just had these developed. I took this one a few nights ago."

The kids were all piled on the boy's top bunk bed just after their bath. Brittany was sandwiched between Jake and Garrett reading their favorite book, *Words of Wisdom for Little Folks*.

"Apparently, I was taking too long to read the boys a bedtime story, and they got Brittany to read to them," I joked. "And Jake"—I pointed at the photo again—"is this not the most adorable picture you've ever seen of him? There's just something about his smile. I don't know. It's different somehow. He looks happier than I've ever seen him."

"They're super cute," John said, "and you're right about how happy Jake looks."

After the picnic, John drove me home to relax for a bit before the evening's activities.

I dropped my keys on the counter and glanced at the answering machine. A wave of panic shot through my body. Five calls displayed on my answering machine. One from EMSA and four from Children's Memorial Hospital. My shoulders tightened and my body froze. I held my breath for a moment before I pressed play.

When the Pain Won't Stop

"This message is for Christy Ennis. This is Dr. Spencer from Children's Hospital. It's urgent that you contact me as soon as possible regarding your sons, Garrett and Jacob Ennis."

My hands trembled as I dialed the number and waited for the doctor to come to the phone.

"I'm afraid I have some bad news," she began. "There's been an accident. Your ex-husband and two sons."

An instantaneous choking feeling rushed up my neck.

Dr. Spencer hesitated and let out a long sigh. "I'm sorry," she began, "Garrett is in critical condition at Children's Hospital and unfortunately, Jacob didn't make it."

I froze, unable to comprehend what I'd heard.

Dr. Spencer's abrupt voice startled me back to reality. "You need to get to Children's Hospital as soon as possible. Report to the ER. Garrett is in room eleven."

Her previous words ricocheted through my mind like pinballs in an arcade game: Unfortunately. Jacob. Didn't. Make it.

I felt like someone had hit me with a stun gun. I rocked my body back and forth as tears dripped on the counter. My baby Jake. Dead. And Garrett—critical condition? Was he going to die, too?

I held my breath and pounded my fist on my leg. "What happened?"

"Their father was driving. He crossed the centerline and hit another truck head on. I'm sorry. Is there someone who can bring you to the hospital? You shouldn't drive."

I stared at the linoleum parquet floor. "My fiancé is here. We're leaving now."

In slow motion, I slammed the phone on the receiver and collapsed on the counter in disbelief. Jake's favorite Power Rangers sippy cup was still on his highchair. Gut wrenching sobs of agony exploded like a geyser.

He would never drink from it again.

When we arrived at the hospital, two police officers stood just outside of Garrett's room.

"Miss Ennis. I'm Officer Harp and this is Officer George. We're sorry for your loss, but we have a few questions before you see your son."

Officer George took out his notepad and recorded my contact information.

"A witness saw Mr. Ennis swerving just before he hit the other driver head on. Are you aware of any previous drug use?"

I clasped my hands over my face and shook.

"Yes, but he's been clean. He seemed fine yesterday when he picked the boys up."

"When the ambulance crew arrived, he was sitting on the curb dazed with nothing on but his underwear."

My eyebrows arched in disbelief. "Nothing? But his underwear?"

"Yes, ma'am. He seemed almost comatose. Oblivious that his children were lying in the street."

John moved forward, his body rigid and his face red. "He didn't try to help Garrett and Jake?"

"I'm not sure. Witnesses saw him disrobe after he got out of the vehicle."

John pulled me closer.

"We did a breathalyzer. Came out clean. But OSBI ordered blood to be drawn to complete a tox screen. The man he hit is in bad shape. He and Mr. Ennis were both transported to Midwest

City Regional."

"And my baby? Where's Jake?"

"His body's been taken to the coroner's office."

"I need...I need to see him!"

"I'm afraid you can't now. Not until after the autopsy."

"An autopsy? For a car wreck? Jake is two! Why would they need to do an autopsy?"

"Standard procedure. It's required for accident victims under the age of three."

"When will I be able to see him?"

"Probably not for a few days."

"A few days?" I sobbed into my cupped hands. "I'm his mother!"

"I'm sorry, Miss Ennis. The coroner will be in touch as soon as you can see him. We've got a lot more to do to finish this investigation." He handed me his card.

Sorrow mixed with frenzied rage. I thought once our divorce was final two years ago, I wouldn't have to deal with Tom's abuse and addiction any more. And his parents—how could they? I couldn't believe they let him get behind the wheel with their grandchildren knowing he was under the influence. Toxicology reports later confirmed Tom was driving under the influence of four narcotics—Xanax, Demerol, Valium and Methadone—as well as Benadryl, an over-the-counter medication known to cause drowsiness. His parents would have to have been blind not to have noticed his crazed behavior.

And now, because of his addiction and their horrific neglect, I'd never hold my baby again. How was it even fair? The guilty one lived. Tom should be the one lying in the morgue.

My teeth clenched and my eyes narrowed in hate. As the sound of the officers' fading footsteps echoed down the hall, my throat tightened and the familiar sting of bitterness wrapped around my anguish.

I was the good parent. I was the responsible one. And now… because of his reckless selfish choices, my innocent baby was gone, and my five-year-old was clinging to life.

I wanted him dead.

I glanced at Garrett's room and shook with angry sobs. "I don't know if I can do this."

The curtain swished open, and the doctor stepped out.

"Miss Ennis?"

I raised my head from John's chest.

"I'm Dr. Mantor," he said, snapping off his latex glove. "Can we have a word?"

A wave of terror shot through me. A word—what did that mean? Good news or bad news? I hesitated, took a deep breath, and followed the doctor into the room. The sight of Garrett was a shock. His jaw and teeth were covered in blood that had now dried a crusty black. It didn't look like he had any teeth left. His right eye was swollen shut, and his mouth was so swollen he couldn't close it. Choking back my fear, I leaned over and kissed his forehead.

"Your son has a fractured jaw and several lacerations on his right leg. We haven't determined if there are any internal injuries. We need to take X-rays." Dr. Mantor nodded at Garrett. "But his jaw is so swollen he can't swallow the contrast dye. We'll have to insert a tube up his nose and into his stomach. Would you like to stay in the room?"

I clenched my hands together and gritted my teeth. What

happened to my peaceful future? What happened to my dreams of sunny days, iced tea, and Adirondack chairs? How would I go on from here?

WHY I'M TELLING YOU MY STORY

Through the pages of this book you'll hear more—the good, the bad and the ugly. How my own insecurities and naivete drew me to toxic relationships in the first place. How the emptiness inside me craved a man to complete me. How my lack of boundaries made me vulnerable to men who would take advantage of me. How my aloneness ached for a man to adore me, yet blinded me to artificial affection and abuse. But most of all, you'll hear about my journey. My journey through healing and the hope it's given me for you to find yours.

It's also important for me to tell you this: I'm not sharing my story so you can feel sorry for me. I'm telling you so you'll know I understand bitterness. I've been best friends with rage. I've experienced the kind of uncontrollable anger that makes you do things you never thought you'd do to escape the agony. I've done things I'm ashamed of just to buy a day of synthetic peace. But as hard as it's been, I've also learned how to release the pain. To forgive the unforgettable. To forgive the unforgivable. Not because my ex-husband deserved it. Not so that he could be free. But because I deserve it. I deserve to be free.

Jake's precious memory lives in my heart every day. The accident that took his life was over twenty years ago. I'll never forget it as long as I live, but I have forgiven. I've escaped the bitterness that held me captive and confiscated my peace. Today, I like me. I no longer feel depleted and miserable, nor do I feel I need a man to fill the vacuum in my soul. Sorrow and regret are gone. Anxiety and rage have dissolved. Panic no longer rules me. I'm comfortable when I'm alone because the emptiness is gone. Today, I'm free.

And that's what I want to show you through this book. I want you to be free. I want you to be confident and joyful, unburdened by the sting of past hurts, disappointments and betrayals. You may not have lost a son, but if you're reading this book, you probably have men you need to forgive. Or, maybe you've forgiven him, but there's a lingering emptiness that won't go away. You're desperate for the pain of the past to evaporate and you just want to feel alive again. Whatever the case may be, whatever you've dealt with, I want you to be free from the weight of your past. Free from the pain inflicted on you. Free from rejection, betrayal, neglect, verbal abuse, sexual abuse, physical abuse, abandonment, rape, and even murder.

Yes, these wounds are harsh. It may not seem possible now to release the appalling anguish. The memories may be brutal and the pain is real. I'm not going to lie and promise you roses. The road to recovery is not easy. It will take dedication and hard work. But your freedom is worth it.

I speak all over the country sharing my story, but I never tell it so others can feel pity. I share my transgressions and sorrow for one reason: to convince you that your freedom is possible. If I found mine, you can find yours too. You may never hear me speak, but through this book I pray you can hear the cry of my heart. Sister, it's time to lay down your bitterness, leave the past behind and discover emotional freedom in relationships. Whether the man you're angry with repents or deserves forgiveness, you deserve to be free. Grab hold of these truths and don't let go. Your new life is waiting.

The road to **recovery** is not easy. It will take dedication and hard work. But your **freedom** is worth it.

- 2 -

What's Poisoning My Soul?

WHETHER IT'S A RELATIONSHIP with a boyfriend, fiancé or spouse, because of the emotional bonds we develop, romantic relationships with men have the capacity to cause the deepest wounds. Yet, it's hard to say how many women struggle with forgiving men. For one thing, many women don't even realize they're angry.

Chewing her nails, Ashley sat in my office with a soft, nervous smile. She met Daniel her first year after college and bent over backwards to please him, but after they got married she discovered he was addicted to porn. At first, instead of confronting him, she denied her anger and tried harder to please him. She made his favorite dinners, lost all her baby weight, and purchased new lingerie. Daniel never noticed.

"Porn ruined our marriage." Ashley blinked back tears. "I can't stop thinking about what he put me through."

Even though they'd been divorced for three years at that point, Ashley still put their wedding album on her coffee table when Daniel came over to pick up the boys. "I've never thought of myself as an angry person, but I guess it's my quiet revenge. It's my way of showing him what he's lost."

What's Poisoning My Soul?

Ashley didn't want to admit her anger, but Amanda didn't know how to let go. Amanda met Kyle her freshman year in college. She told him she wanted to wait until she was married to be intimate. At first he honored her wishes, but a few months into their relationship he started pressuring her to have sex. She got pregnant her junior year. Kyle promised they'd get married as soon as he graduated. Just before Chase was born, however, he broke up with her. Chase is eight and has never met his dad.

"When Chase's birthday rolls around each year, it's a slap in the face," said Amanda. "I get so mad that his dad is not around. I think I've ruined every birthday for Chase because I always end up calling Kyle and leaving a nasty message. I hate it, but I think I've carried resentment for so long it's become my default setting."

For some, a grudge is obvious. An angry scowl. A hateful stare or harsh words. Others feel ashamed of their anger and don't want to admit they're resentful. It's not Christ-like, and they're afraid of what others would think if they really knew how angry they were. Like the extra five pounds concealed by Spanx, they stuff the hurt inside. Repressed anger has a way of oozing out, however, often in physical ailments.

Lisa owned a thriving real estate agency. When she met Jeff, he was flat broke. She fell for his sob story about how his ex-wife took him for all his money, and she let him move in with her. Then she loaned him $25,000 to help him get back on his feet. The next month she came home to find that he had left without a trace. Determined to get even, Lisa hired a private eye and an attorney. "I don't care if it costs more than he owes me," said Lisa. "It's the principle of the thing." Shortly afterward, Lisa developed high blood pressure.

Angela grew up as a middle child and always felt left out. Her brother got all the attention from her father, who spent every spare moment at the football field watching his son play. When she got engaged, her father said he couldn't afford to pay for the wedding even though he had just bought her brother a brand-new truck. Now every time Angela sees her father, she spends a day in bed with severe stomach cramps.

Tiffany's father was a raging alcoholic who beat her when he was drunk. As an adult she sought men she could fix in an unconscious attempt to reconcile her worth. She married another alcoholic, who abused her and refused to seek help. Tiffany's anger turned inward, and she spiraled into despair and depression.

Chelsea's husband took care of the finances. Recently, she found out that they were three months behind on their mortgage and he'd maxed out all their credit cards to build his guitar collection. Soon afterward, Chelsea developed chronic lower back pain that often keeps her in bed. Because of how much work she's missed, she's concerned that she may lose her job.

Tina's husband had multiple affairs. After twelve years of marriage, he left her for her best friend. Once carefree and peaceful, Tina now suffers frequent panic attacks.

Mary found out her husband was gay. He left her for another man after twenty three years of marriage, saying she was never enough for him. Once active physically and socially, Mary stays in bed most days. Recently her doctor diagnosed her with chronic fatigue syndrome.

Like the extra five pounds concealed by Spanx, repressed *anger* has a way of oozing out, often in *physical* ailments.

THE THREE WISE MEN

Boyfriends, husbands, and fathers. These three groups of men have the potential to hurt us more than any other humans can. Perhaps the stories of the women above sound like yours. If so, let me tell you how sorry I am. Injustice and cruelty, betrayal and abuse are unfair. God never intends for any of his daughters to be treated that way.

Unfortunately, these stories you just read are as common in church circles as they are anywhere else. Adversity and suffering know no boundaries. While these stories should anger you, God doesn't want your anger to be contained. He wants you to release it to Him. And there lies the problem.

These women live in dysfunctional chaos because they don't know how to stop the pain. They may have spiritual knowledge about forgiveness, but they lack victory because there's a disconnect. They simply don't know how to release their resentment. It's easier to bury the pain and pretend like everything is okay.

I was like that. From the outside, I looked like I had it all together. I went to church on Sundays and Wednesdays. I went to connect groups and ladies' Bible studies. I memorized scripture. I had verses taped on my mirror and flash cards in my car. I had a massive library of Christian books, cassettes, and DVDs. My house was even decorated with pictures of soaring eagles and chubby little naked angels. I joked at the time that all my coffee cups were saved since they were each embellished with my favorite scriptures.

But with all of my efforts to live right, my soul was a wreck. I knew I was supposed to forgive, but I didn't know how to release the pain. And I know I'm not alone. I've coached women who have held unforgiveness for years before they finally let go.

WHAT'S POISONING MY SOUL?

Magi, one of the women who participated in a small group that studied my first book, *Love Junkies: 7 Steps for Breaking the Toxic Relationship Cycle*, said the following: "I've had so many hang-ups about forgiveness. I've carried a grudge of bitterness for thirty years, but after participating in a Love U discipleship group, I was finally able to let it go. I thank God for putting me into His hands and for using this Bible study to free me!"

Like me, Magi had known she was supposed to forgive, but she hadn't known how.

THE COLD HARD FACTS

Some women have a naturally peaceful attitude that makes it easy to forgive. They love everyone, and nothing ever ruffles their feathers. Maybe these women were born in a baptismal and have Peace & Calming essential oil flowing through their veins. If you're one of those girls, this book probably isn't for you. But the rest of you, keep reading. Personally, I can't relate to women who find forgiveness easy. In my past, I thought hauling around a grudge seemed easier than the work to let go of an offense.

In truth, most of the women I coach struggle with forgiveness. While we may not be able to quantify the percentage, we can make some predictions based on the hurt and sorrow women face as evidenced by other statistics.

- 33% of men have had an extramarital affair.[1]
- 40% of married men watch porn regularly.[2]
- 41-50% of first marriages end in divorce while 60-67% of second marriages end in divorce.[3] (This doesn't consider the women who stay married but are unhappy with their marriage.)

- 39% of women have experienced emotional abuse in a relationship.[4]
- 1 in 5 women are on anti-depressants.[5]
- 1 in 3 women have been physically abused by an intimate partner.[6]
- 18% of women have been raped at some time in their life.[7]
- Nearly 1 in 2 women have experienced sexual violence other than rape in their lifetime.[8]

These figures don't even touch on the emotional trauma and financial ruin caused by addiction issues related to drugs, alcohol, and gambling. Even social media and technology addictions are causing tremendous conflict in relationships.

I'm presenting these statistics to let you know that you're not alone. Other women are struggling with the things you face. Often, when we're hurting, we think no one else is going through what we are. When we isolate, however, it's hard to find the hope and healing we need. The pain of facing our sorrow seems too difficult.

After enduring Luke's drug addiction for eight years, Lauren filed for divorce. The thought of raising four children alone was daunting, but it was better than the insanity and unpredictability of living with addiction. Instead of the peace she'd hoped for, Lauren spiraled into depression. She couldn't stop thinking about everything she'd lost. When Luke got remarried, she lost control.

"I couldn't stand the thought of him being happy when I was miserable. It wasn't fair. I didn't want him back, but I didn't want anyone else to have him either. He put me through hell, and now it was my turn. I was so angry I did anything I could to break up their marriage. My lowest point was when I told his wife that Luke and I had been sleeping together again and that I was pregnant. I never thought about the consequences of my retaliation. It backfired on me when my kids got so upset with me that they wanted to go live with their dad."

Lauren's example may seem outrageous, but bitterness causes us to do things we would normally never consider. "For jealousy arouses a husband's fury, and he will show no mercy when he takes revenge" (Proverbs 6:34). A lot of scripture is written from a man's point of view, and I'm not one to change it up, but I think this verse sums up the sentiments of a lot of women, too. Jealousy arouses a wife's fury as well. Unforgiveness spurs jealousy, and jealousy detonates rage.

Hebrews 12:15 encourages us to get rid of bitterness. "See to it that no one falls short of the grace of God and that no bitter root grows up to cause trouble and defile many."

Maybe you're patting yourself on the shoulder right now thinking, *Wow, I guess I'm not so bad after all. My issues aren't as bad as Lauren's. I would never stoop that low. I may have a little unforgiveness to deal with, but I'm not bitter.*

To say we're bitter sounds harsh and evil. Saying we have unforgiveness sounds watered down and almost spiritually acceptable. Certain words have the ability to soften the blow, but it's time to acknowledge the truth. Unforgiveness may sound softer, but did you know that *unforgiveness* is not really a word? I first discovered this years ago when writing about unforgiveness. Every time I typed the word in a Word document, the program would underline it in red. Many times, I peered at the word perplexed. I knew I spelled it right and was certain I'd caught a major software error. I clicked over to my online dictionary, convinced Mr. Webster would settle the dispute.

I typed in unforgiveness. What popped up on my screen mystified me. Instead of the definition, the words, "Did you mean forgive?" displayed on the screen. I thought Siri was the only one who tried to read my mind with her annoying predictive texting. Now Mr. Webster was playing this game too?

Surely my online Bible would confirm my spelling knowledge. But to my surprise, when I typed the word unforgiveness in www.BlueLetterBible.org the screen displayed, *There are no concordance results for "unforgiveness."* I was stupefied. And apparently stupid as well.

By now I was on a rampage to find out why a word I'd used all my life was not even supposed to be in my vocabulary. I didn't like what I discovered. What so many of us commonly refer to as *unforgiveness* the Bible calls bitterness, rage, and wrath. Ouch. Those words sound ruthless. I'd rather say I'm walking in unforgiveness than to admit I'm bitter or full of rage or wrath. Bitter sounds vicious and mean. Rage sounds malicious and evil. Wrath sounds vindictive and full of cursing. I didn't consider myself to be any of these.

What I found out next was even worse. The Hebrew words for bitterness, rage, and wrath all translate to *poison*.

When I allowed bitterness in my heart, the anger turned to poison inside of me. When I chose not to forgive, it didn't poison my ex-husband, it poisoned me. Anger was hurting me. It was not only robbing me of peace and joy and derailing my emotions, it was hurting my physical body. Remember the women I introduced you to earlier? Lisa developed high blood pressure. Angela suffered severe stomach cramps, and Tiffany struggled with depression. Some may define their conditions as hereditary or coincidence, but when we allow bitterness to move in, the Bible says that we open the door to the enemy.

"In your anger do not sin. Do not let the sun go down while you are still angry, and do not give the devil a foothold" (Ephesians 4:26-27). The word foothold used in this verse comes from a Greek word *topos* which means an inhabited place, a license, a room or a quarter. When we allow bitterness a place in our hearts, we give the devil a room. We give him license to inhabit and permission to occupy. He can't possess a Christian, but he'll gladly come with his troop of terror and start a campaign of oppression and sickness. He progressively gains territory the longer we allow bitterness to stay.

Science confirms what the Bible has been telling us for years. When harbored for a long time "bitterness may forecast patterns of biological dysregulation (a physiological impairment that can affect metabolism, immune response, or organ function) and physical disease."[9]

The link between unforgiveness and illness is startling. God didn't design our physical body to carry bitterness. Bitterness can cause health issues, disease, anxiety, and depression.

Do you struggle with health issues? Consider this. Unforgiveness and bitterness often manifest through sickness and disease. They serve as warning signs alerting us to our need to release offenses.

WHAT UNFORGIVENESS FEELS LIKE

Newlyweds are supposed to be happy, but in my marriage to Tom, I was miserable from the very start. Shortly after the honeymoon, his charming behavior turned abusive and our home became a battleground. For years, I suffered from chronic backaches, Irritable Bowel Syndrome, and several migraines a month. Meanwhile, I'd never been so angry in my life.

I remember one trip to the doctor for a migraine. Tom and I'd had a huge fight the day before about what time he should go to work. We were about to be evicted, and I was livid that he was only working a couple of hours a day. Our daughter, Brittany, was a newborn, and I wasn't back at my job yet. He was in sales and wasn't required to be in the office, and he thought nothing about crawling out of bed around noon. Then he'd sit around and drink coffee for an hour or so. By the time he showered and dressed, it was often three p.m. before he left the house. This only left him a couple of hours to make sales calls. Each night he promised to get up at a decent hour, but each morning he continued to break his promises and sleep in. I was crazy angry. We had daily fights about him going to work earlier.

His empty promises were just the beginning of his abuse. He never had any intention of honoring his word. His promises were his way of exploiting me. I wish I had known then what I know now, that not all domestic abuse is physical and not all forms of abuse, manipulation, and control leave visible scars.

It's often the lack of physical evidence from bruises or blood that leaves women minimizing what has happened to them. You may feel something is wrong, but if you have no scars to prove abuse, you may shrug the idea off and convince yourself that you're overreacting. This is exactly the continuous loop of insanity that can keep you stuck in a vicious cycle of craziness.

Domestic abuse includes many forms of abusive behavior

What's Poisoning My Soul?

including emotional abuse, mental abuse, sexual abuse, spiritual abuse, financial abuse, and, of course, physical abuse. The Office on Violence Against Women defines domestic violence as:

> "a pattern of abusive behavior in any relationship that is used by one partner to gain or maintain power and control over another intimate partner. Domestic violence can be physical, sexual, emotional, economic, or psychological actions or threats of actions that influence another person. This includes any behaviors that intimidate, manipulate, humiliate, isolate, frighten, terrorize, coerce, threaten, blame, hurt, injure, or wound someone."[10]

I realize that talking about abuse can trigger many emotions. While this book is not about domestic abuse, because abuse can cause deep-rooted bitterness, it's important to address what you may have buried. Before we go on, I must say this: if you're a victim of abuse, I urge you to seek the help of a qualified counselor. If you are in danger of physical abuse, find a safe place to stay away from your abuser. It's not enough for him to get help. It's vital that you remove yourself from the situation long enough to find clarity and protect yourself so that you don't go back to the chaos.

"Are you under stress?" my doctor asked the day of my migraine.

"No." The conflict had been the day before. At least the fight was over. Never mind that we may have had another later that day, but in that window of time that I was in his office, I thought I was calm. My stress and anger had become so normal that I failed to recognize it. Of course, not all migraines are due to stress or bitterness, but for me, the buildup of unforgiveness was a huge trigger for my migraines. It was a long time before I would see the connection that bitterness was toxic to my health.

Offenses we refuse to release through forgiveness eventually manifest in our body and can cause a variety of emotional and physical ailments. Physicians can only treat the symptoms with prescriptions and medication, but the Great Physician can eliminate the root through scripture and meditation. It takes a lot of effort and tons of courage, but with God's help we can dig up the roots of bitterness and begin the healing process. The first step is identifying those roots.

PONDER AND PRACTICE

1. When it comes to dealing with your anger how do you typically respond to injustice?
    a. I use quiet revenge. At first I typically deny my anger and try harder to please. But when that fails, I may use quiet revenge to make him pay.
    b. I use vocal revenge. When I'm angry, he's going to hear about it.
    c. I stuff it and try to ignore it. I don't like confrontation and hope the issue will go away.
    d. I try to address the issue before the anger takes root.
2. What physical or emotional ailments cause you distress?
3. Do you think any of them are triggered or intensified by bitterness?

- 3 -

ROOTS OF RESENTMENT

There is an old saying, "Time heals all wounds." I disagree. Time doesn't heal all wounds. Forgiveness does.

ONE DAY WHILE FLIPPING CHANNELS, I saw a commercial for a horror flick featuring mummies wrapped in grave clothes. I'm not fond of scary movies, but something captivated my interest. After the commercial I pressed pause on the remote, and I felt the Lord whisper to me. "Christy, that's you. When you're walking in bitterness, you may be alive, but you're like that mummy. You've allowed offenses to suffocate you. Little by little, layer upon layer, these offenses have spiraled around you like grave clothes. They've twisted around your hands and feet and silenced your voice. They've kept you bound in knots and incapacitated your ability to move on. When you carry the offense, you drag Tom with you everywhere you go. Bitterness is not a weight I intend you to carry."

A strange sensation washed over me. The Lord was right. I was like a mummy. I could barely move. Everywhere I tried to walk, I dragged Tom with me. Invisible shreds of fabric twisted around my soul and anchored the dead weight of his body to mine. I rehearsed angry conversations over and over in my mind. Like an attorney preparing for a case in court, I practiced monologues of bitter laments I wanted to say to him as soon as I got the chance. My mind was consumed with getting revenge, proving myself right, and bringing him to repentance. Instead, my desperate need for vindication and the weight of bitterness prevented me from experiencing my own freedom.

My thumb hovered over the pause button on my remote. I was ready to escape this dialogue. Truth and conviction are unwavering teachers, and I was ready for the recess bell. Instead, a shiver of truth swept through me as I heard the Lord ask me to do something that, up until that point, had felt impossible. "Will you release him to Me?"

To be honest, I wanted to, but I didn't know where to start. Bitterness was a boomerang. Every time I threw it away it came back. Eventually I got tired of the process and gave up. Bitterness kept me bound. It made me miserable. I had lost control of my tongue and my temper. Rage made me do things I didn't want to do in order to find a temporary release from the weight of bitterness.

Acts 8:23 in the NIV says this about what unforgiveness can do to us: "For I see that you are full of bitterness and captive to sin." The NKJV puts it this way: "For I see that you are poisoned by bitterness and bound by iniquity."

Little by little, one strip at a time, the Lord taught me how to unwrap myself from the putrid rags of bitterness. And little by little, the intoxicating freedom of forgiveness changed me. Friend, if that is you, I want you to know this: releasing the pain, releasing that man, releasing the poison of bitterness *is* possible.

The first step to removing the rags of bitterness is to get honest with the resentment we have. We decide we will no longer deny that we're dragging around dead weight. Nor will we be satisfied by merely continuing to manage it or deal with it. So what about you? Are you ready to make a sincere evaluation of any bitterness you may have stuffed, buried, or refused to release? I hope so. Ripping off the grave clothes of unforgiveness is vital to your liberty.

I know I'm not telling you anything you don't already know, at least in theory. It's the practice of forgiving men that evades so many of us. It's like a foreign language we study in school. We can read it, but learning to pronounce the words and become fluent in the speech is a different story.

I don't want you to just know *about* forgiveness. I want you to know *how* to forgive. But first, it's important to identify the rags of bitterness that you may not realize have wrapped around you. When you minimize or bury the pain because it's too difficult to deal with, it doesn't go away. It gets stuffed. Offenses that you refuse to release through forgiveness eventually manifest in your body and can cause a variety of emotional and physical ailments. One day, blood seeps through the rags.

Bitterness and wrath are poisonous and toxic emotions. Psalms 37:8 warns us, "Refrain from anger and turn from wrath; do not fret—it leads only to evil." The word wrath comes from the Hebrew word *chemah*, which translates to fury, rage, venom, and poison. When not released through forgiveness, wrath and bitterness can eventually spread from our emotions to our physical bodies. That's why it's important to pay attention to what your body may be telling you.

The following list of symptoms is not an exhaustive list, but it includes some of the common physical manifestations that may be linked to bitterness. Check the symptoms you experience.

___ migraines

___ frequent tension headaches

___ back aches

___ irritable bowel syndrome

___ high blood pressure

___ nausea or vomiting

___ change in appetite

___ change in sleep patterns

___ neck and shoulder pain

___ hair loss

___ anxiety

___ panic attacks or panic disorder

___ depression

___ jaw clenching or teeth grinding

___ acute stress disorder or PTSD

___ memory loss, confusion, or lack of concentration

Since emotional wounds can manifest in physical symptoms, it's important to find the root cause. That's why the end of this chapter contains an exercise I call the bitterness barometer. The bitterness barometer is a checklist and series of questions intended to help you take a candid look at the men you need to forgive and the offenses you need to release. Like a barometer measures atmospheric pressure to forecast weather and predict storms, this exercise can help you identify the intensity of buried anger that may trigger intense emotional storms.

It's important to evaluate trespasses men have committed against you and appraise your emotions in response to the memory. You're not ripping off the rags to revisit the pain. The truth is this:

Our ***desperate*** need for vindication and the weight of bitterness ***prevent*** us from experiencing our own freedom.

God cannot heal what you continue to conceal. You're ripping off the rags to release the agony and begin your healing journey.

RECOGNIZING BITTERNESS

I once pitched out this question for discussion in a class I was teaching: *How can you tell when you've really forgiven?* I got a lot of great answers but my favorite response was this: "You know you've truly forgiven when the sting is gone—when you no longer feel the emotional charge related to the offense."

Some of us, however, have lived with bitterness for so long we no longer recognize the sting. The emotional charge that we feel in our gut doesn't *feel* like anger. That's because anger can disguise itself in a variety of other emotions like jealousy, shame, disrespect, or disgust, to name a few.

Others manage resentment. We know it's there, but we use coping techniques to keep it under wraps. Like a huge credit card balance we can't afford to pay off, we make the minimum monthly payment and put off dealing with the balance later.

This bitterness barometer will help you identify areas of potential wrath and bitterness. I want to challenge you to be honest with yourself. You'll have plenty of time as you read this book to get rid of all the poisonous venom, but you can't remove the stinger if you continue to ignore it, minimize the pain, or pretend it's not there. Identifying and acknowledging some of these offenses may be painful, so before you begin, I encourage you to find a quiet spot and pray. In fact, may I pray for you now?

Father, I pray for my sister as she takes an honest look at the emotionally intimate and romantic relationships she's had with men who have hurt her and the offenses they have caused. May You hold her hand through this process. May she have the courage to acknowledge every offense, even those that have been buried deep in her soul, and to comprehend your promise for her complete emotional restoration. I thank you that there is no wound, hurt, or offense too big for You to handle, and that You can cause all things to work together for her good. I pray that You will keep her heart safe and that, by the time she finishes her forgiveness journey, she will feel the intoxicating freedom that forgiveness brings. In Jesus' name, we agree together. Amen.

BITTERNESS BAROMETER

Read over the following offenses and place a checkmark by the ones you've suffered. For the offenses you've checked, rate the intensity of resentment or the sting that the memory currently provokes. In other words, if it once angered you but you've worked through forgiveness and it no longer bothers you, circle N for *no more*. If the offense still provokes resentful emotions, circle how often: S for *sometimes*, F for *frequently* or A for *always*.

As you review the scenarios in the lists below, keep in mind other emotions you may feel regarding the offense. For example, the initial sting of the offense or residual effect may feel like hurt, jealousy, rejection, disrespect, anxiety, depression, despair, shame, betrayal, or disgust. These emotions, while not anger per se, may be rooted in unresolved bitterness.

Because issues with romantic relationships and intimate partners often stem from unresolved daddy issues, we will start with taking a look at potential bitterness stemming from our relationships with our fathers.

Look over the following list of offenses and check the ones

that apply to your father. Then note how often the reminders of his actions toward you trigger resentment by circling the appropriate frequency.

N = *no longer* triggered
S = *sometimes* triggered
F = *frequently* triggered
A = *always* triggered

I'm Triggered: *My Father:*

N S F A   ___ was emotionally unavailable
N S F A   ___ was demanding and rude
N S F A   ___ was a harsh disciplinarian
N S F A   ___ left when I was young
N S F A   ___ was not around much
N S F A   ___ was verbally abusive
N S F A   ___ ridiculed, belittled or called me names
N S F A   ___ made me feel ashamed
N S F A   ___ compared me to others
N S F A   ___ was unfaithful to my mother
N S F A   ___ divorced or left my mother
N S F A   ___ was controlling or manipulative
N S F A   ___ was spiritually abusive
N S F A   ___ made me afraid or threatened to harm me
N S F A   ___ sexually abused me
N S F A   ___ failed to protect me

The Roots of Resentment

N S F A ___ abandoned me
N S F A ___ didn't want me
N S F A ___ expressed constant disappointment in me
N S F A ___ committed suicide
N S F A ___ has/had an addiction to drugs, alcohol, porn, gambling, etc.
N S F A ___ has done immoral things

Now look over the following offenses that have may have been present in your dating or marriage relationships. Check the ones that apply and note how often you still feel the sting of resentment by again circling N for *no more*, S for *sometimes*, F for *frequently* or A for *always*.

In dating or marriage relationships, my partner(s) has(have):

N S F A ___ deceived me or lied to me
N S F A ___ told lies about me
N S F A ___ withheld important information from me
N S F A ___ tried to control or manipulate me
N S F A ___ ignored me by an obsessive preoccupation with technology
N S F A ___ cheated on me or committed adultery
N S F A ___ isolated me from friends and family
N S F A ___ addiction issues with pornography
N S F A ___ addiction issues with drugs or alcohol

N	S	F	A	___ issues with other addictions
N	S	F	A	___ left me for another women
N	S	F	A	___ left me for another man
N	S	F	A	___ changed his sexual preference
N	S	F	A	___ verbally abused me
N	S	F	A	___ ridiculed, belittled or called me names
N	S	F	A	___ compared me to others
N	S	F	A	___ constantly criticized me
N	S	F	A	___ twisted God's word to try to control me
N	S	F	A	___ withheld affection to try to control me
N	S	F	A	___ used money to control or oppress me
N	S	F	A	___ financially drained me
N	S	F	A	___ abandoned me
N	S	F	A	___ made me afraid
N	S	F	A	___ threatened to harm me
N	S	F	A	___ physically abused me
N	S	F	A	___ sexually abused me
N	S	F	A	___ forced me to do things I didn't want to do
N	S	F	A	___ allowed others to abuse me
N	S	F	A	___ raped me
N	S	F	A	___ stole from me

Evaluating Your Responses

Look over the offenses you checked, paying special attention to the ones in which you frequently or always feel resentful. These are the offenses you'll want to focus on releasing as you continue reading this book. I also want you to look at the offenses in which you sometimes feel resentful. It's normal to feel resentful occasionally as we reprocess our emotions when memories resurface. However, whether you checked sometimes, frequently or always, it's important to be honest with what you do when you feel resentment again.

When those emotions resurface, how do you typically react?
Check all that apply:
___ forgive again and release the offender
___ hold onto the bitterness and refuse to forgive
___ enjoy the attention and pity from others
___ stuff the bitterness
___ deny the hurt
___ use sarcasm
___ try to get even or retaliate
___ provoke the other person to anger in order to minimize your own
___ go shopping
___ overeat
___ restrict your food intake
___ use alcohol to cope
___ use drugs to cope
___ indulge in inappropriate behavior or other addictions to mask the pain
___ engage in self-harm

Resentment can be an explosive emotion; anger is only one letter away from danger. If there are several areas in which you always feel resentful, this book may not be enough. I'd encourage you to consider whether a professional counselor could help you as well.

ACTION STEPS

Find a Trusted Prayer Partner or Mentor

We confess our sins to God so we can be forgiven, but we confess our sins to one another so we can be healed (James 5:16). None of us can walk this journey alone. We are called to pray for one another and bear one another's burdens. Find another woman you trust. Share your struggles with forgiveness and ask her to hold you accountable and pray for you. There is great healing and emotional support that comes from prayer and fellowship with godly women we trust.

Journal Your Prayers

Journaling is a great tool to help you on this forgiveness journey. Use your journal to start a dialogue with God. Find some time when you're not rushed to record your thoughts, prayers, and questions about anyone you need to forgive. Then, listen for the still small voice of His reply. Don't reduce your prayer to a monologue. Prayer means communion with God, and the King of the universe longs to talk to you. You can ask Him anything. His word promises that He's always with you (Psalms 139) and that as you call to Him, He will tell you great and unsearchable things (Jeremiah 33:3).

- 4 -

Counterfeit Comforters

Bitterness is a poison. The only antidote is forgiveness.

MY HEAD THROBBED AS MY HAND pounded the alarm clock to stop its assault. Too many drinks the night before, and it was only Wednesday. Flashbacks of the previous evening floated across my mind. Vodka gimlets in the hotel lobby. Three… or was it four? Dancing. Then he walked me to my room.

I crawled out of bed and squeezed drops of Visine into my bloodshot eyes. As I swallowed three Advil, I caught a reflection of myself in the mirror. Instead of a look of disgust, an odd response washed over me—relief. I smiled at the face in the mirror, and for the first time in months I felt liberated. I felt justified. My affair? As far as I was concerned, my husband deserved it. If he'd treated me right, I wouldn't have needed another man's arms to help me escape my prison of bitterness.

I drove to work with the sunroof open and the music blaring. The high was exhilarating. A stranger's embrace consumed my thoughts as I reimagined our first dance to one of my favorite songs, *She's Like the Wind*. I turned up the volume even higher and breathed in the crisp October air. My anger was gone.

For a couple of weeks, my euphoria remained heightened as I fixated on fantasies of our next time together. But he never called, and I soon discovered the reality of addiction. My affair had only been a temporary anesthesia to numb the pain of my bitterness. The high from my one-night stand had only offered momentary relief.

Now what? Desperate, I felt trapped between the abyss of my own misery and the promise of the next high.

He wasn't hard to find.

It was a lot easier the next time. After a little experience with guilt management, the weight of shame wasn't as bad as I'd thought it would be. As long as I balanced it out with huge doses of justification.

He started it. Our astronomical telephone bill for his calls for phone sex along with his pornography addiction are proof of his unfaithfulness. He brought this sin into our marriage. I didn't. Besides that, he's not honoring me or cherishing me. His drug use has destroyed my trust, and his work ethic has nearly bankrupted us. How am I supposed to respond to a man I no longer respect?

The aftermath of the second affair, however, left me even more desperate than before. More was not enough. I needed increasing doses to maintain the same level of comfort.

An old flame was my next temptation. (Siri calls him Tim Tation.)

A few months later, I sat in my pastor's office. Counseling was supposed to help our marriage, but as far as I could tell nothing had changed. Most of the time my husband failed to show up. Such was the case that particular day. My face was hot with rage when I blurted out to Pastor Dan, "I'm having an affair with my old college boyfriend."

I didn't confess because I wanted forgiveness. I confessed the situation, not my transgression. I didn't want my pastor's advice or counsel. I only wanted him to fix Tom. The affair was evidence of how desperate I'd become to find relief and of how broken our marriage was. If he could fix Tom, I could be whole. Wasn't that his job?

PAIN MANAGEMENT

When men hurt, abandon, and betray us, women often turn to anything that will stop the pain. Some mask the pain. Some minimize the pain, and others maximize it. I call these pain management styles the three M&M's. Some women mask their bitterness by indulging in excess work, exercise, food, drugs, alcohol, recreation, social media, shopping, and even other relationships just to provide relief. Other women stuff and minimize their hurt by denying it altogether. Still others maximize their pain in order to draw in attention and consolation. All three escape strategies, however, blind women to the fact that bitterness is a poison. These pain management strategies suspend the only remedy—forgiveness.

THE MASKERS

Maybe you're like I once was. I thought it was easier to cover my pain or bury it altogether. At first my tactics seemed innocent. Shopping trips—or retail therapy, as I like to call it—seemed effective to console my sorrow after a fight with Tom. But when the conflicts in our marriage increased, the relief shopping provided no longer soothed me. I needed something better, something stronger.

My first affair caught me off guard. The enemy strategized and waited for an opportune time. For months he'd taunted me with thoughts like, "You deserve better than Tom." And then it happened. Out of town on a business trip, I stopped in the hotel lobby for happy hour.

A few drinks on a swivel barstool. A few flirtatious smiles. A few dances.

One great big hook.

The one-night stand was like a cocaine rush, and soon I was trapped in a vicious cycle I couldn't stop. My affairs were like addictive pain killers. The word addiction is not in the Bible, but the book of Ephesians describes my indulgence as a continual lust for more (Ephesians 4:19). That pegged my behavior. I wanted to stop, but I didn't know how.

In desperation I indulged in impurity to cover my hurt. I was a masker. So effective at masking my pain, I also denied any responsibility for my actions. Like Eve, I cast the blame. The affairs were not my fault. The Apostle Paul must have been talking to me when he wrote, "For I see that you are poisoned by bitterness and bound by iniquity" (Acts 8:23 NKJV).

Yep. That was me. Held captive to my sin.

Kim's story has similarities to mine. Kim and Carl had been married for thirteen years. "I loved Carl with all my heart," Kim said, "but his addiction to pornography was more than I could bear. Even after he found freedom and healing, I couldn't forget the past. I was constantly badgering him and checking up on him. I didn't know how to forgive."

Kim married within a year after their divorce was final. "I needed another man to stop the bleeding in my heart. At first, things were great, but it didn't take long for the bitterness to bleed through. Our marriage lasted only a year and a half."

After Kim's second divorce, she cried out to God for comfort. It wasn't easy, but He led her on a journey of releasing her bitterness and forgiving Carl. "I realized that until I forgave Carl, another relationship wouldn't remove my bitterness."

A couple of years later, Kim and Carl remarried. Today, their marriage is stronger than ever. Kim leads a connection group for women, where she uses the pain of her past to encourage other women out of their own bitterness.

FROM FURIOUS TO CURIOUS

After seeing "Flashdance" at the age of ten, Robia Scott knew what she wanted to do—be a dancer. With passion and drive she pursued her goal with fury, and by the age of sixteen she landed in Hollywood. Throughout the next twenty years, Robia's career as a professional dancer and actress afforded her the opportunity to work with the recording artist Prince and star in numerous television shows like Beverly Hills 90210, CSI, and Buffy the Vampire Slayer.

From the outside it looked as if she had it all, but something was missing. Inside she was tormented. "My deepest desire was to find freedom, to be at rest and feel at ease with myself and my life," said Robia.

Instead of fortune and fame, however, Robia's life revolved around counterfeit comforts. Food, cigarettes, clothing, and her appearance. Obsessed with what she ate, how she looked, and what she weighed, Robia was miserable.

"I spent years looking for answers," she said. "But one day, while sitting in a casting office waiting for an audition, a woman with the words I AM tattooed on her neck went to get a drink from the water fountain."

"I was curious. I thought the tattoo had something to do with new age religions, so I asked her about it." The girl explained that I AM was a name that God gave himself in the Bible when he introduced himself to Moses at the burning bush. Intrigued, Robia went to church with her new friend, and a few weeks later she gave her life to Christ.

A conversation at the water fountain led to a conversion of faith. The Great I AM was the comforter Robia had been looking for.

It didn't happen overnight, but as Robia grew in her relationship with God, she eventually walked away from a thriving career in the entertainment industry and entered full-time ministry.

In her book, *Counterfeit Comforts, Freedom for the Imposters That Keep you from True Peace, Purpose and Passion*, Robia Scott says this about her recovery: "The Lord showed me that whenever I felt rejected, sad or disappointed, I did not go to the Holy Spirit for comfort, but to Mrs. Fields' cookies or to my good friends Ben and Jerry. (Chocolate fudge brownie ice cream, in particular.) I had developed a habit of running to something—anything—but primarily food for an emotional release or to numb out so I wouldn't have to feel anything at all."

One day Robia heard the Lord whisper this in her spirit: "You do not have a food issue. You have a feelings issue."[11]

That's just like God. He doesn't beat around the bush. He goes straight for the root.

Your back story and my back story may not be the same as Robia's. I've never struggled with food issues, but I have struggled with feelings. And it's not until we dig up the root that our true healing can manifest. If we only deal with the surface issues, the root grows back, stronger and more powerful than it was before.

I've used my own brand of counterfeit comforters to conceal my injuries. I've used relationships as an escape from my misery. I've buried anger. I've stuffed the hot coals of bitterness until my soul was one spark away from a volcanic explosion.

Trying to deny my need for a relationship would not take care of the root of my issues. No, my issues went deeper. My affairs were only the surface sin. Controlling symptoms never heals. It only prolongs the problem. In the meantime, the issues grow and multiply.

In Luke chapter four, a Samaritan woman met the Great I AM at the water fountain, too. And her conversation with the Messiah led to her conversion of faith. When she recognized true peace, the woman at the well dropped her counterfeit comforters, the promiscuous relationships that she'd used to shield her pain. When she chose to let go, she found her freedom, and she became a credible witness. Her encounter with Christ eliminated her need for any other comforter. She became the world's first female evangelist.

I AM was the comforter she was looking for.

Speaking of female evangelists, remember earlier when I mentioned that Robia walked away from the entertainment industry? Apparently, God had other plans. As the Great I AM would have it, He wove her acting skills back into her ministry. In a divine twist of events, Robia met the writers of the hit film, *God's Not Dead*, and was invited to audition for a role in their next project, *Unplanned*. When Robia landed the leading role of Cheryl, the clinic director of *Planned Parenthood*, she knew this was a great opportunity to shift culture and usher in a new mindset. God twisted the pain of her past into a beautiful plot of purpose.

It's not until we dig up the **root** that true **healing** can manifest.

THE MINIMIZERS

Like I once did and like Kim and Robia once did, many women mask their pain and bitterness by running to counterfeit comforters that promise relief. They know they're supposed to forgive, but the process of forgiving is often too vague. It seems easier to bury and deny the pain.

Instead of running to God and releasing the offense, they squash their emotions with anything that provides temporary relief. For some women, however, masking the pain fails to provide relief. For them, the easiest way to forgo forgiveness is to deny that they're even angry in the first place.

They minimize their pain with a variety of lies in order to delay action or rationalize their anguish. They buy into their lies in order to reject reality and numb the crazy. They minimize, compromise, and tell themselves things like:

- I'm not angry.
- It's normal to feel pain in love.
- I can change him.
- He's really not that bad.
- He doesn't mean to do the things he does.
- He *says* he's a Christian.

When women remain stuck in this unhealthy pattern of denying the pain, they're often propelled by more lies:

- It's all my fault.
- There's something wrong with me.
- This is the best I can do.
- I deserve this.

Minimizing, rationalizing, and denying our pain also makes us unaware of the bitterness that begins to grow. Often, we don't recognize bitterness because it manifests as shame, guilt, and self-condemnation. Other people can also contribute to our denial. Although their advice may be well intended, their comments can influence our perception and delay our acknowledgement of the offense and the resulting forgiveness. Their comments can also produce shame and other feelings of self-hatred. We may wonder why we are so conflicted when others make comments like:

- Get over it.
- It's not that big of a deal.
- You shouldn't feel that way.
- You asked for it.
- You should have known better.

The Bible warns us about people who dish out false comfort. "They dress the wound of my people as though it were not serious. 'Peace, peace,' they say, when there is no peace" (Jeremiah 6:14). The NASB puts it this way: "They have healed the brokenness of My people superficially." Be careful whom you listen to. Everyone has an opinion, but not everyone offers wise counsel.

THE MAGNIFIERS

Not all women run to counterfeit comforters to mask or minimize the pain. Some prefer counterfeit comforters to magnify the pain by soliciting pity from others. They nurse their wounds by maintaining a victim's mentality and draw others into their web of misery. They don't want to get better. Magnifying their hardships and nursing their wounds justifies their bitterness and prevents their need to forgive.

Tiffany's first marriage ended after her husband's compulsive spending habits led to a foreclosure on their home. "It was a nightmare—creditors calling all the time. I didn't deserve it. I've worked hard all my life and had plenty in savings when we married. I wasn't going to put up with his junk anymore."

Tiffany seemed to thrive on talking about the past. Instead of masking her pain, she preferred to magnify it. She thrived on the attention her misery produced. She'd tell the same stories over and over of how wronged she'd been when her ex-husband "took her for a trip down foreclosure lane." Ten years after their divorce, she still talked about it as if it had just happened recently to anyone who would listen. Tiffany didn't want to get better. She preferred to stay bitter. For her, the only way to manage the bitterness was to cover it with the doses of comfort and compassion she extracted from others.

Every time she heard, "Girl, I'd be mad, too!" or "He deserved what he got!" she felt endorsed and validated. There was no need to address her bitterness as long as she felt entitled to it. She gravitated toward people who provided false compassion. They listened to her complain and murmur. Like the prophet Zechariah said, some told her what she wanted to hear.

Some people prey on those who are vulnerable. They enjoy being sought out for advice, but the advice they give is superficial (Zechariah 10:2). They comfort others in vain and provide false comfort so that the wounded will keep coming back for more.

If someone tried to encourage Tiffany about her need to forgive and release the past and all of its offenses, she'd raise her voice and complain louder. Those people offering truth tired of her constant complaints. They figured out she didn't want their advice. She only wanted them to endorse her misery. Tiffany often grumbled that her friendships were short lived. New acquaintances would do the fade-out by taking longer to answer texts or phone calls. They were spent. But when Tiffany exhausted one source of comfort, she sought out another unsuspecting victim.

WHEN PAIN BECOMES A TROPHY

My friend, Lyn, broke her wrist on vacation one year. She and her family had gone on a four-wheeling expedition and on the last turn, her navigation skills didn't cooperate with the terrain. She came back from the doctor sporting a bright pink cast which she embellished with rhinestones. "As long as I have to wear this thing, it may as well be cute," she said with a grin. True to tradition, she also collected friends' autographs on her cast.

Lyn enjoyed the consolation from friends who were sorry about her accident, but six weeks later when the doctor removed her cast, her healing was complete, and the commiseration ceased. Compassion is necessary, but it has a season.

Tiffany's attitude was like Lyn's. She enjoyed the compassion she received from friends who consoled her when they heard about her suffering. Only Tiffany never went back to the doctor. Her fracture may have been invisible, but it was permanent. She wore her offense with pride like a pink rhinestone-studded cast, milking attention wherever she went. Whenever someone listened to her story and validated her pain, it was as if they were autographing her broken arm.

The attention she received redirected her focus. As long as Tiffany magnified the offense, she was unable to forgive. Instead of burying the pain, she elevated it. Instead of removing the splinter, she put a cast on it and wore it where ever she went. Her pain became a trophy.

RESIST REVENGE

A few years ago, a popular country artist sang a song aimed at a girl who rejected him in high school. After he achieved success, he sang, "How do you like me now?" It's been said that revenge is sweet. But oh, the price. Planning payback creates a temporary solace, but like a mirage, it never satisfies. It's a horrid haven that creates a barrier to forgiveness. If your mind is consumed with getting even, bitterness is the motivator.

When Eric left her for a woman half her age, Rebecca wanted to get even. "I didn't want him back, but I wanted him miserable," she said. "I became obsessed with doing whatever I could to make him regret the day he let me go. Everything I posted on Facebook was for his benefit. From glamorous selfies to photos at fancy restaurants with a new guy every weekend, I wore myself out trying to make him want me back."

When we take revenge, we not only blind ourselves to bitterness, we hinder divine justice and leave no room for God's wrath (Romans 12:19).

In the book of Esther, one of the king's noble's, an evil man named Haman, convinced the king to sign a law to kill the entire Jewish nation. He did this unaware that Queen Esther was a Jew.

Planning **payback** creates a temporary solace, but like a **mirage** it never satisfies.

(Esther had kept her nationality a secret because her uncle Mordecai had asked her to.) She resisted the urge to retaliate and instead prayed and waited on God's vengeance. As a result, Haman's evil plan was discovered, and he was hung on the very gallows he'd had built for Mordecai.

Because Esther didn't take the matter into her own hands, a divine reversal was set in motion that didn't stop at Haman's death. In a dramatic turnabout for fair play, Mordecai moved into the palace and was given Haman's estate. Talk about a sovereign sanction. Next time you think about giving an eye for an eye, remember how faithful God was with Esther. Let her story be proof that God's ways are higher than yours. Selfish strategies to seek justice only lead to disorder and destroy our own peace (James 3:16).

A counterfeit comforter is like a pacifier. It starts out in innocence. At first it whispers a false promise. *Use this and you'll be free of pain.* But counterfeit comforters can only mask the pain. They can't eliminate it. Instead, these counterfeits become addictions that bring destruction and lead to our demise. Weaning ourselves from things that only bring temporary relief is like taking a pacifier out of a baby's mouth. There'll be lots of screams, but it's the only way to reach maturity.

God makes us a promise when we relinquish our rights to His authority—to bring peace that will produce a harvest of righteousness.

THE REMEDY

The remedy for relief is not found in synthetic comforters but in releasing the offender. It's only when we choose forgiveness that we have the capacity to receive lasting peace. Jesus said, "I am leaving you with a gift—peace of mind and heart. And the peace I give is a gift the world cannot give. So don't be troubled or afraid" (John 14:27 NLT). When we forgive, we receive His gift of freedom—a peace that surrounds us like a shield. But, when we harbor bitterness, it repels our liberty. Just like water and oil don't mix, peace cannot coexist with bitterness.

God promises to comfort us in all of our troubles (2 Corinthians 1:3-4). The word comfort used in the New Testament comes from the Greek word, *parakaleō,* which means to call to one's side, to speak to, to exhort, entreat, comfort and instruct, to console, encourage and strengthen, to instruct and teach.

Forgiveness opens the door for divine comfort. When we call on God for help, He comes to our side. He instructs and encourages us. He provides the strength we need to overcome our hurts, wounds and offenses. He instructs and teaches us how to release them to find our freedom. He wants us to come to him with everything, all our pain and suffering.

Like Robia discovered, He is the Great I AM. He's not the Great I WAS or the Great I WILL. The Great I AM is the comforter, the healer, the counselor. He is authentic, the real deal. He is genuine. Like the chart on the next page depicts, counterfeit comforters are no match for the comfort of the Great I AM.

PONDER AND PRACTICE

1. Which of the pain management styles most characterize your responses to pain? Why do you think that is?

COUNTERFEIT COMFORTERS

  a. I mask: I indulge in other things to cover the pain or bury it.
  b. I minimize: I tend to stuff it and deny it altogether.
  c. I maximize: I tend to amplify the issue in order to get sympathy.
2. Look over the characteristics of counterfeit comforters in the chart below. Which symptoms aggravate you the most?
3. Notice the corresponding attributes of forgiveness. How do these benefits motivate you to throw away your counterfeit comforters?

A COUNTERFEIT COMFORTER:	FORGIVENESS:
Produces fear	Produces peace
Keeps you bound	Sets you free
Destroys strength	Increases your power
Cannot heal	Restores and heals
Is deceptive	Tells the truth
Is habit forming	Breaks bad habits
Hardens your heart (Ephesians 4:18)	Softens your heart
Is never enough	Is always sufficient
Acts like a mirage and keeps the freedom from pain just beyond your reach	Acts like a mirror showing you the root so you can remove it
Pushes down pain and allows bitterness to grow undetected	Elevates the pain so it can be removed

- 5 -

Father Wounds

MY FATHER WAS NEVER AN affectionate man. As long as I can remember, he seemed detached and disinterested in anything that involved me.

Dad grew up in the depression era, a culture typified by handshakes and formalities. A society where emotions were best kept in little black boxes full of secrets tucked away forever. Appearances were prized. Failures and fears were contained, not expressed. Happiness was hushed. And for my dad, I-love-you's were never spoken.

I craved love, but, as a young girl, I never experienced it. In my teens, I made a vow with myself. As soon as I was old enough to date, I would find love. I wasn't sure what I was looking for, but I was convinced it involved a disco ball and a cute cocktail with its very own paper umbrella.

And a fake ID.

I saw it on television. The formula for romance was spelled out in perfect detail. Every Friday night at seven o'clock, I sprawled out on the shag carpet with a bowl of popcorn for one hour of strategic planning.

Watching "The Love Boat" ladies gave me hope. They'd sit on a swivel barstool and smile, tossing back their feathered bangs. After a few sips of a pretty pink drink, Mr. handsome would magically appear. They'd dance the night away, and before the cruise was over, she'd hear the words that I was desperate to hear.

You're beautiful.

You mean so much to me.

I love you.

I couldn't afford to go on a cruise, but I was sure I knew where I could find a disco ball.

CARS AND CIGARS

I was a junior in college when my mother dragged my father to my sorority house for a visit. He was dressed in a red V-neck sweater that Aunt Mary got him for Christmas and some brown polyester slacks. Except for the small hole in his pants from a cigar burn, he looked handsome.

And fatherly.

It wasn't often that I saw him out of coveralls. When I was growing up, as soon as he got home from work, he took off his leisure suit and tie and went to the garage to tinker on one of his cars.

Dad loved cars. And cigars. I was hoping that his visit that day meant that he also loved me.

He fidgeted in his pants' pocket and pulled out his lighter.

"John, you can't light that thing here!" my mother scolded.

We stood on the veranda of the sorority house. I watched him while he twisted his Swisher Sweets cigar in his mouth, sucking on the butt like a lollipop. He took it out for a moment and glanced at me. "What's your major, Chrissie?"

My mother gasped in disgust and brushed imaginary crumbs off her dress. My heart dropped. *He doesn't know? How could he be that detached from his only daughter's life?*

With my father's full disclosure of his disinterest, my suspicions had nowhere to hide. I had spent a lifetime trying to make him notice me, but now it was obvious: I still didn't matter.

Unworthiness, insecurity, and shame had been squatters for twenty years. That day, they became permanent residents.

THE HURTS WE BURY

Just like an untreated wound can cause complications and spread infection to other parts of the body, unhealed wounds from our fathers create toxic emotions. These buried hurts cause internal strife and create obstacles to intimacy in almost every subsequent romantic relationship until we deal with the festering wound.

It's hard, however, to deal with a wound we don't recognize. Daddy issues have a way of burying themselves so deep that many of us don't realize they're there. We've lived with a vague feeling that something is missing for so long, we think it's normal. We may think everyone feels the way we feel. Everyone feels this void. Or maybe we recognize the emptiness and conclude that there must be something wrong with us—that we are unlovable. We're unworthy. We're inadequate.

Daddy issues are the root of many of our grown-up problems. Maybe you had an emotionally unavailable father like I did. If so, you probably understand that just because your father was present in the home doesn't mean you felt his affection. Some men don't know how to express love.

Maybe you never knew your father. Maybe he subjected you to abuse or abandoned you through neglect or imprisonment. If that is you, please know how sorry I am. God does not wink at these atrocities.

Until we come to a place of forgiveness with our father wounds, however, we're left with few options. We either distance ourselves emotionally or we physically walk away from an irreparable relationship with our father. Or, like a giant magnet, the abandonment, abuse or rejection compels us to seek validation, either from the one who rejected us or from a replacement we deem suitable. In our efforts to reconcile the injustice, we jump through all kinds of hoops in order to prove the abuser wrong and restore our identity.

Such was the case with Meghan. Meghan's mother was raped as a freshman in college. Her mother didn't know her rapist, and he was never caught.

"I feel like a part of me is missing," said Meghan. "I loathe what he did, but it's odd. As much as I despise what he did, there's an unexplainable longing in me to know him. The craving for my father's love has led me to many compromises. Most of my relationships have been with men who are emotionally unavailable. I think I'm subconsciously drawn to men who will reject me. It's like I'm trying to win their love in order to reverse the rejection and prove my worth. To get it right this time."

Neglect, abuse and abandonment cause deep wounds, but divorce, drug addiction, and death can also fracture or terminate our relationships with our fathers. Manda knows this full well.

As a young girl Manda adored her father. "I was his sidekick, definitely a daddy's girl. I followed him everywhere, and he called me his 'cupcake'," said Manda. "When I was about five, I started noticing that my dad was sick a lot. I'd beg him to play with me or dance with me, but he always said he didn't feel good. I was too young to understand anything about drug addiction.

"I was eight when my parents divorced after my father had a few failed stints at drug rehab. When my dad moved back to Oklahoma, fifteen hundred miles away, I was devastated. After that, the only type of communication we ever had was a phone call. Everything was so confusing. All I knew was that my dad wasn't around, and I didn't know how to deal with the despair. I started bottling my feelings because I felt so alone, as if I didn't fit in anywhere. Middle school was when all crap hit the fan. I was the tomboy. I felt like everyone else was prettier, skinnier, or richer. In eighth grade I started cutting.

"My mom found out, and I did get some help, but the pain didn't stop. My dad continued to disappoint me. Throughout the next several years, I could tell with the first few words of a phone conversation whether he was sober or messed up. Of course, he'd always lie and say he was sober.

"When I was thirteen, one Sunday evening at eleven p.m., a police officer knocked on our door with the horrible news that my father had passed away. His death certificate stated that the cause of death was accidental suicide by drug overdose. That's when the hole in my heart burst wide open. The now permanent absence of my father left me shattered. I felt bitter and betrayed.

"A couple of years later, I started dating my first boyfriend. At first things were great, but gradually things shifted. He talked me into doing things I never thought I'd do, and I tolerated things I never thought I'd tolerate. He never hit me, but the mental, verbal, emotional, and sexual abuse I suffered were unbearable. I was angry, yet I didn't know how to stop him. I was too scared and desperate for love to do anything about it."[12]

It would be years before Manda would realize how the absence of her father's love set her up to make bad relationship decisions. The familiarity of misery was like a boomerang. The vacancy of her father's love enslaved her in the sorrow she wanted so badly to escape.

Whatever your daddy issues may be, when a woman doesn't feel the love of her father, she will often seek love elsewhere or find an escape for her pain. Little did I know that the void in my own heart would be a magnet to draw me to series of abusive relationships. I had yet to discover that brokenness attracts brokenness.

CAPTIVATED BY CHARM

When I first met Tom, I was enthralled by his charm. He told the most captivating stories, embellishing every detail with more grandiosity than Times Square at Christmas. I listened for hours, elated and relieved to finally have a man interested in me. My desperation for love blinded me to the reality that I never got a turn to speak. I merely served as his audience. He was so needy that there was no room for me, but I was to broken too notice.

We were married for ten years. Ten years of lying and deceit, manipulation and broken promises. Ten years of drug abuse and pornography addiction. Ten years of dodging creditors due to financial issues related to his drug addiction. Ten years of twisted threats:

If you ever leave me, I promise you'll regret it.

You're a piece of trash. No one will ever want you.

God will curse you if you file for divorce. I've consulted with my attorney. Trust me—you'll never see your children again.

Tom's threats had no foundation, yet, with his trademark mixture of rage and charm, he deceived me into belief. He kept me in constant confusion by weaving empty vows between his ruthless threats:

I'm so sorry for the pain I've caused, but I've changed. I promise, if you give me one more chance, I'll be the man you've always wanted.

I've quit doing drugs and have a great job now. The past is behind us. Now, it's our time to have the marriage we've always wanted.

You know you'll never find another man who will love you like I do.

His promises were gilded vows. Like a dime-store necklace in a black velvet box, they sounded real, but underneath the thin veneer of 14kt gold was nothing but cheap talk.

MY CONCRETE CASTLE

I breathed a sigh of relief after I'd blurted out the truth. As I straightened my hunter green skirt, I glanced at Pastor Dan, trying to assess the look on his face. Was he shocked about my affairs? Or had he suspected that I'd been involved with someone else? It didn't matter. Now that my secret was out, it felt good to have someone share the burden of my misery. Someone who could now help me fix Tom and put my marriage on the right path.

Pastor Dan leaned forward in his leather chair. His elbows seemed glued to his cherry wood desk as he clasped his hands under his chin and looked me straight in the eye.

"Christy, I understand that you're hurting and that Tom's behavior has caused tremendous problems in your marriage. I know you probably don't want to hear this, but I'm concerned that if you don't confess this to Tom, you will never get free."

My mouth fell open, and I threw my hands in the air. *Are you kidding me? Was that all he had to say? Who was going to fix Tom?*

"Oh, gosh." I grabbed my face. "I know what I'm doing isn't right. But Tom!" I inhaled and held my breath in frustration. "He's the one driving me to do this!"

Holding firm to my belief that the problems in our marriage were all Tom's fault, I left Pastor Dan's office that November day with no intention of confessing. A few weeks later, however, Tom had an individual session with Pastor Dan. I knew my pastor would not betray my confidence, but he didn't have to.

Tom was having suspicions and asked Pastor if I was having an affair. Pastor Dan replied with an empty stare. He neither acknowledged nor refuted Tom's inquiry, but Pastor Dan's silence screamed.

Tom knew.

Later that afternoon, I heard footsteps coming up the stairs to our second-floor apartment. They were quick and heavy. The keys rattled in the door, and Tom flung it open and slammed it so hard that the Oriental picture on the wall swung back and forth. I saw a fury on his face I'd never seen before.

"You're having an affair"—he grabbed my arm—"aren't you?"

His face was inches from mine. His pupils were constricted, and I could smell his breath. It reeked from whatever drugs he was on.

Pushing his arm away, I glared at him with frozen lips.

He staggered back toward me with eyes full of rage. "Is that what you've been doing on your so-called business trips?"

"Oh, so you think you're the saint?" I yelled. "I don't know a woman alive that would put up with you."

"So you're admitting it? Who is he?" Tom reached for the phone. "I'm calling him right now. What's the jerk's number?"

"I'm not admitting anything except that I can't take this marriage anymore!"

"Well, I don't need your confession. Pastor Dan told me everything."

I sobbed as my body fell in a heap on the couch. I was done with the masquerade. I could no longer deny the truth. Caving under the pressure, I waved the white flag. I admitted my guilt but blamed Tom for everything. I still wasn't sorry. I just wanted the battle to be over.

The day my affairs were disclosed was the worst day of my life. It felt like my world evaporated. I was left with no reprieve from my prison of bitterness.

The concrete castle I'd built to protect myself from the chaos in my marriage crumbled. I had nowhere to turn but to God. I didn't know whether He'd forgive me or banish me to hell, but it didn't take long for me to discover the truth.

My earthy father would show no mercy. I could hear him now. "You should've known better. I told you he was a con artist. You should've listened to me."

But my heavenly Father was different. Despite my behavior, despite my choices, He never rejected me. He'd been waiting for me to get to the end of myself. He'd been waiting for me to need Him. He'd been waiting for me with open arms.

THE KEZAZAH

Friend, you may have not made the same choices I made to anesthetize your misery. But I hope you can relate to the desperation I felt to find relief.

I don't think there's a woman alive who is content to live without her father's love. When we don't receive it from our earthly fathers, our daddy issues will drive us to seek it elsewhere. When the elsewheres fail us, a desperation sets in until we exhaust all of our own efforts to seek relief.

Jesus told a story about someone I can relate to, the prodigal son. It's too bad this tale isn't about the prodigal daughter. It would fit so much better in this book, but I think you'll get the point just the same.

In this familiar story, the son of a wealthy man demands his inheritance early. He didn't want to wait until his father passed away. In essence, demanding it early was the same as saying, "You're dead to me." It was the ultimate rejection and act of rebellion.

The son knew what he was doing. But for whatever reason, he didn't care. He thought he could make it on his own. His departure didn't go unnoticed. His father's house was in a community. In order to leave, the son had to walk past all the villagers. All the neighbors knew.

He knew by leaving he would never be able to return. Such prideful actions were considered so disgraceful that the Hebrew culture had a ceremony for any deviants who tried to return home. It was called a kezazah. When the prodigal tried to come home, the community would gather around him. They would break a large pot in front of him and shout, "You are cut off from your people. You are no longer considered part of this family."

The son packed his bags anyway. He took the money and ran. He was willing to reject everything he knew to try to live life his own way.

The word prodigal means extravagant wastefulness or an overindulgence in sensory pleasures. I can relate to this guy. I didn't have a wealthy father, but I've been guilty of overindulgence and lavish living to cover my misery. I'm not sure about you, but if you've ever overindulged in something, I bet it was to compensate for something that was missing. Jesus doesn't say what the prodigal son was missing, but he was bent on covering the pain. Most versions of this story indicate that the son spent his money on prostitutes and liquor. He probably did, but according to this definition, there are numerous ways we can act like a prodigal.

Some of our indulgences can start out innocently. We can overindulge in guiltless things like hobbies and work. Shopping and social activities. Sports or social media. It's not always the activity that's wrong. It's the overuse to medicate our pain. It's using something as a crutch instead of reaching out to Christ.

Often, our prodigal behavior and overindulgence to conceal our pain are obvious to everyone else, but invisible to us. Such was my case. I blamed my shameful behavior on Tom.

The prodigal son was filled with pride, but that pride wasn't evident to him until all his money was gone, when the ATM denied his transaction, when his credit cards were all maxed out.

He was greedy. It wasn't until his money was gone, until he was bankrupt both physically and spiritually, that he finally felt his need. Wealth was his vanity crutch—the thing he took pride in, the thing that enabled him to walk confidently, the thing that made it possible for him to indulge every wish and desire. His vanity crutch was his money, and, once it ran out, he could no longer walk.

When he wound up with nothing, he got to the end of himself and came to his senses. That's when he crawled back to his father.

When my vanity crutch—my adulterous relationships—were

no longer able to provide relief, I, too, came to my senses and crawled back to my Father.

The son expected to be met by a community ceremony. He expected to be put on the reject registry. He expected his father to deny him. He expected to live as a slave. He expected his community to defile his presence with a kezazah, labeling him as unworthy. Like the prodigal son, I expected to be scorned and shamed by my Father.

But that's not what happened for either of us. The father ran after both of us...with open arms.

How

grateful

I am.

And even more so when I understood why Jesus specifically mentioned that the father ran.

Jesus often taught in parables or stories that illustrated the point he was trying to make. Many of the stories have greater meaning when we understand Hebrew customs. In their culture, it was considered shameful for older men to run or to show their legs. That's why it's so impactful that the father ran. In order for him to get to his son, he would have had to gather his tunic to free his legs and run past all the villagers, who would be staring in shock at his disgraceful actions. But because of his great love, he was willing to violate social statutes and cultural commands in order to bear the shame of his son.

He ran past the villagers. With every slap of his sandal on the dusty ground, his legs communicated, "I'm taking my son's shame. Put your pots away! There will be NO KEZAZAH!"

Likewise, your heavenly Father is running after you. He doesn't care who's looking. All he cares about is making sure that you know how much He loves you. No matter how many times your earthly father has ignored, abused, or rejected you, God's love can cover every hurt. And no matter what you've done to bury your pain, He's willing to take all of your shame.

Friend, wherever you are, your heavenly Father is waiting for you with open arms. He doesn't reject you or shame you. No matter what you've done, his love screams…

"There will be no kezazah."

No matter what you've done, his *love* screams... there will be no *kezazah!*

- 6 -

Defeating a Victim Mentality

I'M ABOUT TO MAKE a shocking statement. Are you ready? It may not be what you want to hear, but here goes: Not all infirmities are the result of physical issues.

I know what you're probably thinking. Seriously, Christy. How can you say that? You're not a doctor! No, I didn't rush out and get a medical degree, but I'm basing this statement on the story of the man Jesus healed at the pool of Bethesda. The man had been lame for thirty-eight years. Lame was weak and crippled, but the reason he was bound was due to his own sin. Lame wasn't born that way. He got bound that way. His weakness grew from a seed of rebellion that eventually manifested in physical ailments until he could no longer walk.

And like so many of us, when Lame didn't get better, it was easier to blame his condition on others. Sin and blame create a noose that keeps us bound. Some for life. For this man—thirty-eight years before Jesus arrived.

When Jesus saw Lame at the pool and learned that he'd been that way for a long time, he asked him a very strange question. "Do you want to get well?"

Defeating a Victim's Mentality

Jesus does that a lot.

Asks obvious questions.

It's not like he doesn't know the answer. But he does it on purpose—to draw out the real issue. The answer should have been obvious. An emphatic "yes" was the correct reply. But Jesus' question didn't get the expected response. To Lame, yes was no longer an option. Living in defeat, he blamed his situation on others.

Thirty-eight years of failure had caused him to adopt a victim's mentality. It was easier to blame others for his condition than to get up and walk away from his issues. Eventually Lame accepted his condition as his fate and blamed others for his bondage.

The 5th chapter of John tells the story beginning in verse two.

Now there is in Jerusalem near the Sheep Gate a pool, which in Aramaic is called Bethesda and which is surrounded by five covered colonnades. Here a great number of disabled people used to lie—the blind, the lame, the paralyzed. One who was there had been an invalid for thirty-eight years (John 5:2-3,5).

The word, invalid used in this verse comes from the Greek word *astheneia*, which means a weakness, not only in the body, but a weakness of the soul. It also means a frailty to bear trials and troubles, a want of strength to restrain corrupt desires.

Our English word, *asthenia*, originates from the Greek. Asthenia means a lack or loss of strength, an abnormal loss of strength. Maybe you've felt like an invalid in some areas of your life. I know I have. And while it's not a fun place to be, there is good news. If strength can be lost, it means it once was there to begin with.

Jesus looked at Lame. His words echoed. "Do you want to get well?"

Lame hung his head low and frowned as he traced his fingers on a seashell. "I have no one to help me get into the pool," he lamented. "Every time I try to get in, someone else pushes me out of the way."

Maybe others sympathized with him. Maybe he traded the attention his handicap received for the hope of recovery. After all, sympathy was easy to get.

Hope was remote.

But Jesus didn't register Lame's complaint. Ignoring his misery, he spoke with unusual authority.

"Get up!" Jesus commanded.

Startled, Lame lifted his chin. Squinting in the sunlight, he stared at the stranger kneeling beside him. *Excuse me? Who are you to talk to me this way?* He must have thought. *Can't you see that I'm crippled? Where's your compassion?*

Jesus could have consoled his pain and just put a Band-Aid on his issue. But Jesus refused to validate the invalid. He knew that empathy given to one bound by sin would only tighten the knots. Instead, he offered the hope and healing that truth brings. His words may have seemed harsh, but like antiseptic on a fresh wound, truth always stings before it brings healing.

"Pick up your mat and walk," he demanded.

Curious, Lame straightened a bit. He was used to others endorsing his misery. But this man was different. For the first time in thirty-eight years, someone expected him to take responsibility for his handicap. This man spoke with authority, ignoring his excuses.

Lame glanced at Jesus, searching for sympathy, but Jesus' gaze didn't budge.

Lame looked around. By now others were staring.

He sat up and drew his knees to his side.

This guy is going to look foolish when I try to get up and just fall

Defeating a Victim's Mentality

back down, he thought.

Cautious, he stood. Surprised, he noticed his legs were solid. He took one step and then another. A thousand thoughts flooded his mind.

Is it really true? Am I really healed?

Like a newborn calf emerging from the womb, he twirled and galloped around while the crowd watched in amazement.

"I'm healed! I can walk!" His eyes danced in wonder as he skipped along the shore. The pool of Bethesda was no longer his home.

That's when Jesus slipped away into the crowd.

Later, Jesus found Lame at the temple. Notice the word *found*. Jesus hunted him down a second time. The Savior of the world went looking for Lame, and when he found him, he said, "See, you are well again."

Again...hmm. Meaning Lame had once been well. And what Jesus says next reveals what brought on his weakness and infirmity in the first place: "Stop sinning or something worse may happen to you."

I love the story of Lame because it shows us that Jesus will find us even in our sin. Jesus knew that Lame's sin crippled him and gave him a victim's mentality. But he didn't wait for Lame to cry out. Instead, Jesus went to find him. He hunted him down at the pool of Bethesda. He offered hope and healing before Lame even asked. Likewise, Jesus will heal you before you ask. But like Lame, your healing won't manifest until you stand up in faith.

Our issues continue to be a handicap when we refuse to take responsibility. They keep us bound when we continue to sin. But once we stand up, Jesus offers hope and healing to us all.

We never heard what Lame's sin was. Maybe it was something we'd classify as one of the biggies, but maybe it was simple. Maybe it was a lack of trust. Maybe it was a refusal to move. Maybe it was blame.

Has Jesus been hunting you down? If so, I imagine he's asking you the same question. "Do you want to get well?"

If so, pick up your mat and walk.

Not all infirmities are the result of physical issues. Likewise, not all bondage is the fault of others. Some of our bondage is self-inflicted. Sometimes we go willingly into our prisons. And that's what the rest of this book is about—showing you how to ditch the victim mentality. Showing you how to pick up your mat and walk away. Far, far away from the crippling effects of anger and bitterness.

And dance on to your own place of freedom.

IDENTIFYNG MENTAL HANDICAPS

Like Lame, unless we decide to pick up our mats and walk, we'll remain seated in a pool of misery. That's what bitterness is. Like strands of invisible seaweed slithering around us while we wallow in sorrow, the slime of bitterness is sleazy. So as hard as it is, we're going to take a look at how our mental handicaps contribute to our misery.

A mental handicap is a false belief, behavior, or attitude that predisposes us to toxic relationships. The resulting conflicts compromise our ability to forgive. When our slate is full of offenses, we live on a merry-go-round of misdeeds, often resorting to blame tactics to ignore or deny our responsibility.

We play the blame game when we say things like:

"It's his fault I'm crippled or damaged, or _____."

"I've always been this way. I can't change now."

"It's too hard."

And like Lame lamented, "I have no one to help me."

It may be hard to recognize and identify our mental handicaps, but it's a vital step in our voyage from misery to freedom. We can't heal from what we refuse to acknowledge.

We may have no control over some of the ways others offend us, but many of those offenses we've allowed are because we have weak boundaries and have permitted unacceptable behavior to continue. Often our anger and bitterness are the result of things we *can* change—unrecognized mental handicaps. Part of laying down the blame is identifying our own weaknesses, which draw us to unhealthy relationships in the first place, and therefore create an environment where bitterness has potential to flourish.

Everyone has weaknesses, so before we go on, let me say this: weaknesses are not wrong. Everyone has areas where they're vulnerable. When we identify our areas of vulnerability, we can either work to eliminate them or put guards in place to protect us from them.

Let's use insurance as an example. We purchase a policy to protect against a risk that is more than what we're capable of handling. Policies are all about minimizing risk. We evaluate risk and cover it. For instance, most of us could not withstand the financial burden that would come with the loss of a home, say to fire or flood, so we purchase insurance to protect ourselves.

There are ways to protect ourselves from relationship risks as well. Part of protecting ourselves comes from accepting our past mistakes and refusing to make them again. The other part is acknowledging our handicaps. Denying they exist keeps us bound

Our *issues* continue to be a *handicap* when we refuse to take responsibility.

in a cycle of self-defeat. Becoming self-aware, however, can help us pursue healthy patterns of behavior. Admitting our part in the cycle of bitterness is a quantum leap into our recovery. This difficult but necessary stride is the first step to laying down the blame so we can find our path to healing.

Below is my list of the most common mental handicaps that can keep us bound in bitterness and stuck in the blame game. Taking note of the ones you struggle with will help promote self-awareness. When you're aware of your weaknesses, you can put plans in place to eliminate them or minimize their effects.

HAVING UNRESOLVED ANGER ISSUES

Mandi expressed some profound self-awareness at a codependency meeting I once attended. "I used to wonder," she said, "did I pick the wrong person?" She paused for a moment and shifted in her chair. "The truth is, any guy would have been the wrong one. In the shape I was in—until I learned how to put my past behind me and forgive my father—my anger and bitterness issues would have either drawn me to unhealthy partners or caused me to destroy even a healthy relationship."

Mandi had identified her handicap. She recognized that her own anger was the root of her inability to enjoy a healthy relationship. Like Mandi, until we recognize our part and hold ourselves accountable to change, our handicaps will keep us bound in misery. And then, even if we pick the right guy, our bitterness will cause us to sabotage what could have been a healthy relationship.

Our bitterness is like a heat-seeking missile—a weapon with an invisible guidance system that seems to draw us toward explosive targets. When we're bitter, we're bound and held captive to oppression and injustice (Acts 8:23).

PICKING MEN YOU WANT TO CHANGE

This is what I did in my marriage to Tom. I fell in love with his potential. My lack of self-confidence convinced me that I didn't deserve the kind of man I really wanted, so I settled. I fell for a fixer-upper—a man I wanted to change and mold to reflect my desires. But try as I might, Tom didn't want to be fixed.

It took me a long time to realize the truth. When it comes to relationships, what you see is what you get. A fixer-upper is only a good investment if it involves real estate and land, not a man. You can tear down a house to the studs and remodel it, but the walls that support a man's character are often built with sheets of steel. They don't come down easily.

IGNORING RED FLAGS

Some of the best dating advice I've ever heard came from a kindergarten teacher. Before crossing the street she told her students, "Stop, look, and listen." Likewise, before you cross the road into a new relationship, stop, look, and listen. Pay attention to behavior and watch for the red flags. But what's even more important? Watch for the yellow flags.

Yellow flags always come first. Before a traffic light turns red, the yellow light warns drivers to slow down. But truth be known, what do most of us do when we see a yellow light? We stomp on the gas pedal and gun it! And that's where we get into trouble with relationships.

When we ignore the yellow flags, we hurry past the places where we should exercise caution. We may notice concerning behavior; but, instead of slowing down, we accelerate, full speed ahead with heart-pumping excitement. This behavior causes us to miss the more subtle warning signs. When you first meet a new guy, it's important to be ultra-cautious. In the beginning of a relationship, you're only meeting his personal representative. Only time will tell if who he initially seems to be is an authentic portrayal of his real person and character. Chanel's story is a good example of what I mean.

Why You Should Order a Drink on a Date

Chanel, the daughter of my friend, Tammy, recently broke up with someone she'd been dating for a few months who seemed like a great guy. Isaac was an engineer with an established career and an impressive salary. He owned his own home and attended church—all must-have requirements for Chanel. And, at the age of 31, Isaac said he was ready to settle down.

"He seemed like the kind of guy dreams are made of," said Tammy. "But I was suspicious. I had to wonder...where's the catch?"

The first clue surfaced the evening Chanel introduced Isaac to her parents. During a casual conversation about football, his abrupt change of topic seemed awkward and out of place.

"I'm fasting from beer," he announced.

Hmm. That's an interesting thing to mention out of the blue, thought Tammy.

"Not that I have an issue with beer," he continued.

The additional disclaimer put Tammy on high alert. She knew

that a defensive disclosure usually meant the opposite. She wondered, *why is he so sweaty? It's not even hot outside. And why are his hands shaking?*

Tammy knew from experience with her brother's alcoholism that those were signs of withdrawal.

"You need to be aware and watch his behavior," Tammy told her daughter later. "Alcoholics go to great lengths to hide their addiction."

Then Tammy gave Chanel some atypical advice.

Even though Chanel seldom drank, Tammy encouraged her to order a drink whenever she and Isaac went out to eat or were at social functions. She wanted to give Chanel an opportunity to observe how he handled his liquor. At first Isaac drank moderately. He was still trying to prove himself and win Chanel. When men are in a mindset of pursuit, they don't let down their guard until an emotional engagement seems secure. As soon as he felt Chanel had fallen for him, his drinking got out of hand.

After just a couple of months, Isaac often showed up drunk for dates and chugged several beers at dinner. When his behavior got belligerent, Chanel videoed him to confront him later when he was sober. Another time, while he was passed out on her couch, she investigated further. Looking at his cell phone, she learned he'd been texting other women when he got drunk and she wasn't around.

While I normally would've never thought to encourage a woman to drink with a potential love interest, this ended up being great advice. I'd like to offer another option, however. If you don't drink or are in a recovery program, don't compromise your own ethics or sobriety. You can always order a virgin cocktail. The mere suggestion of alcohol can create conversation about your views and open dialogue. It can also expose reality if he perceives that your drink is an invitation for him to indulge. Then you can make observations about how he handles his liquor while staying completely sober yourself.

If Chanel had never tested this issue to observe his behavior, Isaac may have succeeded in concealing his alcoholism. Like Chanel almost did, many women ignore yellow flags in relationships and don't discover the red flags until after they've either become so emotionally connected that they can't release the relationship or until after they tie the knot.

If you have concerns about yellow flags, put your heart on hold. Then, find a safe way to evaluate your concerns about unacceptable character traits and potentially deal-breaking behaviors.

GETTING EMOTIONALLY INVOLVED TOO SOON

The initial high of romance creates blind spots that hinder our ability to see things in proper perspective. Connecting emotionally too soon is dangerous because our emotional involvement clouds our ability to assess a man's character.

Why do we do this? Because women are emotional beings. Most of us long for a man to cherish us. Now, don't get me wrong: there's nothing wrong with our emotions. God wants us to be emotionally connected. That is one of the most beautiful blessings a marriage can have. But the greatest asset you own is your heart; giving it to someone who is unable to cherish it is dangerous.

Proverbs 4:23 says, "Above all else, guard your heart, for everything you do flows from it." We have a responsibility to protect our hearts by making sure that those we allow entrance are worthy of our affection. One of the biggest mistakes women make in a new relationship, however, is believing everything a guy says and jumping in emotionally. That's playing Russian roulette with your heart. My advice: don't put stock in anything he says yet. Let his words go in one ear and out the other. In the beginning, you're in a watch-and-wait mode.

That may sound judgmental, but here's why it's so important: the vast majority of communication is non-verbal. In other words, most of what we communicate is read through gestures, facial expressions, posture, and tone of voice. While you may be quite discerning about these types of nonverbal cues, there's so much more to consider. What about his character, behavior, and motives? Those can't be verbalized. Character and motives must be observed and validated under the lens of adversity. A piece of glass can look like a diamond, but it will shatter under pressure. A genuine diamond won't.

Likewise, the only way to determine whether or not a man is displaying genuine character or just putting on a good show is to observe how he responds to difficulties. Watch how he reacts to the irritations of life. Does he have grace or blow up? Is he patient or demanding? Does he blame or take responsibility when he's at fault? Is he courteous when rebuked or does he take offense?

Before we give our hearts away and allow a man to have full access to our emotions, we have to evaluate whether or not he is sincere. There's no fast way to do this. True intentions and character take time to evaluate.

Even lenders, employers, insurance companies, and non-profits know this. You can't go to a bank and tell the loan officer that you're a suitable candidate for a mortgage. It doesn't matter how much you try to convince her that your credit karma is high, she's going to pull your report. You can't apply for a job and insist to the interviewer that you're qualified. You'll need to fill out an application and submit a resume. You may even be asked to pee in a cup while they check your references.

Insurance companies don't charge everyone the same premium. They evaluate their risk based on how many claims you've had. In some cases, you can't even volunteer at a church program without submitting to a background check. Churches have a responsibility to ensure that those who work with their members, children, and youth are safe. All these organizations evaluate character to protect their assets.

Your heart is an asset. And it is worth more than rubies. You are the only one who can protect it. It's up to *you* to guard your heart. Don't give it away to the first guy who tells you that you're the one he's been looking for all his life. Don't be gullible. The way you guard your heart is to watch him. Watch him closely. Listen to the way he talks about his mom, his employer, his ex. If he disrespects them, guess who may be next? Watch and wait. Watch to see if his actions align with what comes out of his mouth. And my best advice is this: Wait for something bad to happen.

Wait for something bad to happen? I know what you're thinking. Why would I want to do that? Because you want to see how he reacts when things don't go his way. Any guy can keep his game on when he's winning. It's only when issues arise, when adversity comes, when things don't go his way, that the *real* man stands up. When he's squeezed, the real man is revealed.

That's why wise women wait. They pay more attention to actions and give less credit to words until they can appraise whether or not a man's words are genuine.

True character is a lot like underwear. We may assume everyone wears some, but it's only when they bend over that we can tell for sure. So don't make assumptions about your guy's intentions. Watch his actions and behavior. Don't get emotionally involved until you've witnessed evidence of genuine character.

LACKING SELF-CONFIDENCE

It's been said that opposites attract, but when it comes to our emotional health and self-confidence, we attract who we are. In other words, our emotional health is like a magnet, attracting us to those with whom we're emotionally compatible. We may not have the same emotional vulnerabilities, but like an outlet and an electrical plug, we fit together to provide each other the energy we need.

Steve was all about Steve. He was used to being the center of attention, and when he wasn't in the limelight, he created a spotlight with his charm and humor. On the outside, he appeared confident, but his confidence did not come from within. Instead he drew his emotional energy from the applause of others.

Jennifer was quiet, cautious, and compliant. Unsure of herself, her lack of self-confidence drew her to men who validated her with attention and flattery. So when Steve amped up the charm and complimented her daily at work about her clothing and style, she was smitten. Her coworkers warned her about his flirtatious ways with women at the office. His own obsessive need to be the center of attention made him pursue several women at once. But it was too late. Jennifer felt a special connection and responded with warmth to Steve's advances. In her eyes, he could do no wrong.

Defeating a Victim's Mentality

Steve and Jennifer both had emotional handicaps that drew them to each other. Steve's need to feel idolized fit like a glove with Jennifer's need to be pursued to prove her worth. When Jennifer grew weary of Steve's insatiable need for adoration, he began flirting with other women in order to fulfill his need for attention. When the flirting turned into an affair, Jennifer broke it off. Her self-confidence, however, took another beating, and the emotional drain from the breakup validated her unworthiness.

BEING TOO NICE

Anyone ever tell you you're *too* nice? You may be an enabler. Do you pick up the slack and assume your partner's responsibilities? Do you often do for him what he's capable of doing and should do for himself? If so, maybe it's because you feel sorry for him. Maybe you feel guilty. Or maybe pride causes you to manage his load because you feel you can do it better.

Some of us have too much empathy. We lack boundaries. We pride ourselves on our patience. But too much patience is not good. In fact, Naisha learned that too much patience is detrimental to a relationship.

Naisha thought Nate was her white picket fence and happily-ever-after, but two years into her marriage she discovered Nate had racked up over $6,000 in credit card debt she hadn't known about.

Nate seemed repentant and apologetic. He cancelled his credit cards and gave Naisha his passwords to his accounts so she could monitor his agreement to pay it off. Naisha even took on more hours at work to help Nate with the payments.

Three months later, Naisha went home for lunch and checked the mail. A new credit card statement had arrived. This bill was for $3,500. In tears, she confronted Nate. Unable to deny the proof, Nate did what he always did—profusely apologized, admitted he was wrong, and promised he'd never do it again. This was the last time.

Instead of holding Nate responsible for his actions, Naisha made excuses for him. She convinced herself that he didn't mean to put their financial well-being in jeopardy. He didn't have a lot of money growing up, but he knew better now, and he was on the verge of a breakthrough. She sold her wedding ring to pay off the bill, confident that Nate's remorse was genuine.

It wasn't long before trouble came again. Naisha was livid when she received a phone call one day from their mortgage lender. Nate was three months behind on their house payment, and their home had been referred to foreclosure. With all the attorney's fees and late charges, Nate only had half of the money to reinstate the mortgage. Naisha was so angry she filed for divorce.

Patience is a good thing, but too much patience is destructive to a relationship. When we allow men to avoid taking responsibility for their actions, we not only deprive them of the opportunity to build their character, we also set ourselves up for the bitterness that is bound to come when they disappoint us again.

HAVING A VICTIM MENTALITY

It's important that we recognize our vulnerabilities. When we're ignorant of our weaknesses, we are powerless to protect ourselves.

Naisha's experience taught her that her enabling led to bitterness. After her divorce, she joined a recovery group for codependency. "The group helped me learn how to set healthy boundaries in relationships," said Naisha. "I always thought I was a caring person, but my care came with a lot of expectations. That wasn't genuine care. My expectations were a form of control. As long as others did what I expected, everything was fine. But when they didn't meet my expectations, bitterness began to consume me. Now, when my nature to help comes with a funny feeling in my gut, I realize I need to stop. Otherwise, if I say yes when I really want to say no, I'll end up dealing with a mess of bitterness later."

Like Naisha learned, ignorance is not bliss. And like Lame learned, refusing to move and blaming others for our situation keeps us bound in a cycle of self-defeat. Becoming self-aware, however, helps us pursue healthy patterns of behavior.

Laying down the blame and discarding our mental handicaps positions us to release the bondage of bitterness. We're changed when we can look back, disentangle the blame, and begin to see the pain of our past turned into purpose for the future. And that's what Part Two, *The Freedom Blueprint*, is all about. I'm anxious to show you how you can build a healthy foundation for your soul by developing eight freedom essentials. When you apply these principles, you'll develop personal strength and confidence, and the pain of your past will lose its power. Are you ready? It's time to move beyond brokenness and find freedom for your soul.

PART 2

THE FREEDOM BLUEPRINT

> *"Earth is forgiveness school. It begins with forgiving yourself — then you might as well start at the dinner table."*
> *Ann Lamott*

SO FAR, WE'VE TALKED A LOT about how bitterness affects us and why it's important to forgive. We all know that. It's the application that's difficult. That's why the second half of this book will take us on a journey that will show us the progressive nature of forgiveness.

Forgiveness is hard. It's a lot like algebra. We can't learn how to solve an algebraic equation until we've learned how to add, subtract, multiply, and divide. These are the prerequisite skill sets that must be learned first. Likewise, there are principles we need to have in place before we can resolve our forgiveness equations.

Step-by-step we'll learn how to increase our capacity to exercise forgiveness through what I call the *Freedom Blueprint*. We'll learn how to strengthen our souls by developing eight essential freedom skills that will enable us to forgive and make it stick.

Because it doesn't always stick.

How many times have you forgiven someone and then, a few

PART TWO: THE FREEDOM BLUEPRINT

days later, found yourself angry all over again? Somehow, bitterness found a crack and made its way back. It's like a boomerang. We may toss it away, but it knows where to find us.

Like the dust bunnies we swept away last week.

Forgiveness is not a one-and-done experience. It's something we have to do over and over again. It's kind of like cleaning house. We can't clean house once a year and expect it to stay pristine. Neither can our spiritual houses stay free of offenses if we only examine ourselves once a year.

When the disciples asked Jesus how many times they should forgive their brother, he replied with a mathematical equation: seventy times seven. For those of you who think He meant there's a limit to how many times we are to forgive, that's not what Jesus was saying. The Greek translation doesn't mean 490. It means *countless*.

What Jesus was saying is that there's no limit to how many times we should forgive. We are to forgive to infinity and beyond. Jesus knew His father remembered our sins no more (Isaiah 43:25). If God doesn't keep tally, neither should we keep a record of those who trespass against us. Jesus knew how important it was for his followers to release offenses. Bitterness is one of the biggest ways we sabotage our freedom. When we don't forgive, we can't be forgiven. Plus, it poisons *our* soul, not the souls of our offender.

YOU ARE GOD'S CASTLE

Are you ready? In Part Two, you'll get into the nitty gritty and move beyond the *rules* about forgiveness and learn how to use *tools* to move past the pain and into your place of freedom. You'll learn mindfulness strategies that will help you break down the vague concept of forgiving and letting go into a series of progressive action steps that will help you live a life that's fully present. You'll find the confidence and freedom you're meant to have.

By using castle architecture to illustrate the scriptural truth that you are the temple of God (1 Corinthians 6:19), the following chapters will help you complete a building inspection to make sure your palace is up to code. One nail at a time, you'll study the blueprint of a healthy castle to ensure yours is equipped to destroy the sting of the past and keep your heart strong and full of joy.

The Freedom Blueprint details eight freedom essentials and takes an in-depth look at building a healthy foundation for your soul where freedom and forgiveness can flourish. In the following

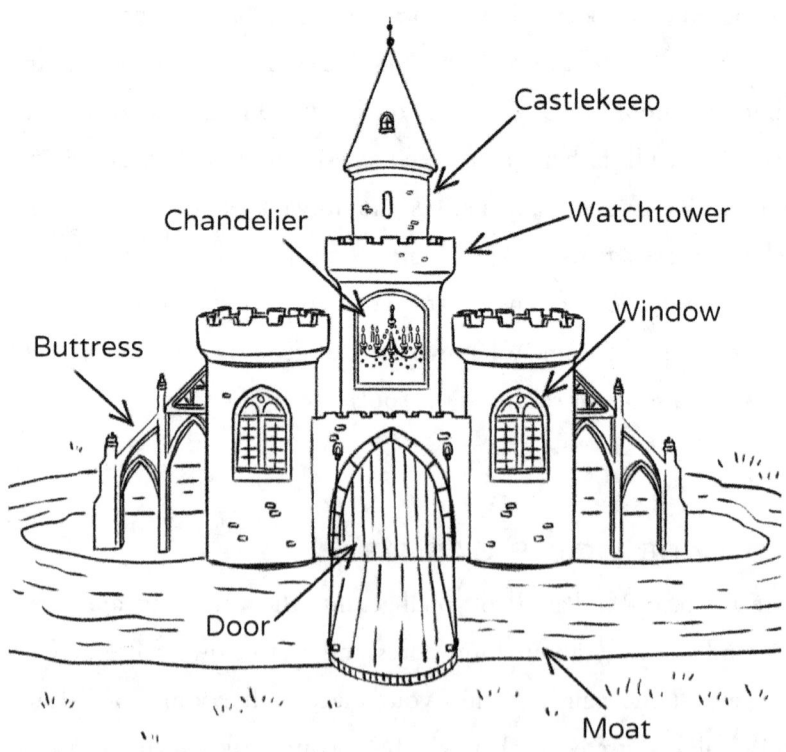

PART TWO: THE FREEDOM BLUEPRINT

chapters you'll learn the importance of ensuring that your castle has functioning:

Windows to help you identify how the enemy is gaining access to your castle with bitterness and betrayal.

Doors so you can decide what thoughts you want to give permission to enter.

A moat to help you gain confidence with setting boundaries, in particular with learning how to say no. You'll receive suggested responses to a variety of situations and guidelines to help you decide if a man who has betrayed or hurt you is worthy of your trust again.

Chandeliers to illuminate your castle with the light of the Holy Spirit so you can feel God's presence surrounding you.

Buttresses to add support with the scriptural benefits of forgiveness as well as identify the side effects of bitterness. This section will also address several false beliefs you may have about forgiveness, bringing clarity to ideas like, "Forgiveness means he's off the hook," or "Forgiving means we have to reconcile."

A watchtower to help you pay attention to the divine whispers that God reveals to you through your circumstances, ideas, and intuition. You'll also be encouraged to ask God for His perspective on what you've endured and the plans He has to prosper you.

A castle keep—a castle within the castle—designed to be a secure place of refuge during war. Like a safe room, the keep is the most secure part of the castle. When you enter this stronghold, you'll learn how to depend on God and stay protected from the voice of Satan, the voice of culture, and the voice of reason.

A crown of authority to access the sovereign power that God has set aside for you.

Even when the sting of betrayal seems impossible for you to

forgive, you'll learn that with each freedom essential you develop, you'll gain personal strength and be one step closer to the confidence you desire.

When you apply these principles, step-by-step, you'll learn healthy responses to the hurtful things men have done. You'll be able to remove the sting of the past, regain your confidence, and laugh in the face of the future.

Let's get started! In the next chapter we'll talk about how to install windows so we can start to shut down the enemy's strategy to gain access to our castle.

PART TWO: THE FREEDOM BLUEPRINT

WANT TO STEP IT UP A NOTCH?

Let Go & Thrive is an online coaching group developed as a companion to Part Two of *Free Looks Good on You*. Learn and grow together with me and a small group of like-minded women.

Let Go & Thrive will help you if:

- You're tired of the drama in your marriage or dating life.
- You want a stronger identity in Christ.
- You want step-by-step help with forgiving.
- You're tired of the emotional roller coaster of relationship ups and downs and are ready to invest in YOU.

Relying on your circumstances or your partner to change is futile. That's why it's so important for you to take charge of your life. Your spiritual and emotional health is the most important element in maintaining your peace and joy as well as determining relationship success.

Here's more of what Let Go & Thrive will cover:

- False beliefs about forgiveness.
- How you can find freedom through forgiveness even when he does nothing to deserve it.
- How you can forgive...even if he never changes.
- How to get your confidence back. We'll talk about tearing down the idol of other people's opinion (it's a slippery slope) and learn how to put your hope, confidence and trust in God.
- Emotional boundaries: How to implement them and why you need them.
- Prerequisites for forgiveness. Did you even know there were some?
- Evaluating relationship risk. Yes you can! I'll show you how and it's not judging. It's looking for evidence of character and paying attention to the yellow flags. Yellow ones always come first!
- Should you trust him?
- Becoming stronger and loving YOU.

If you're ready to leave the past behind and find emotional freedom in relationships, you can find out more at https://www.christyjohnson.org/let-go-and-thrive/.

- 7 -

Looking Back to Look Out

CAN YOU IMAGINE A HOUSE without windows? Sunshine would never have a chance to dance through your curtains in the morning and kiss you hello. Gentle breezes would never be able to deliver fresh air. And without a way to look outside, how would you ever know if someone was trying to get in?

Every house needs a way to look outside. Windows give us access to what is going on around us. Windows allow us to see beyond the perimeter of our castle. If we're under attack or blindsided by circumstances on a continual basis, it may be because we've never looked out the window.

Here's the deal. If you can't see where the enemy is gaining access to your castle, he'll keep coming back in the same way. He won't stop until his plot no longer works. You've got to be smarter than he is. Like an investigative reporter, you've got to learn what to look for.

The devil has a plan of attack. He has strategized schemes. What works for your friend may not work for you. The way he invades her fortress may be different than the scheme he's created to vandalize your abode. That's because we all have unique vulnerabilities based on our personalities, maturity, and life experiences.

Military strategists create detailed plans to infiltrate their enemy's property. Bank robbers study blueprints to find out where the bank is vulnerable. Football coaches watch video upon video. Frame by frame in slow motion, they study the other team's plays as well as the weaknesses of their players in order to develop a game plan to outmaneuver or overpower their opponent.

And guess what? You're no different. Somebody's watching you. If you don't know where your castle is vulnerable, how will you be able to install reinforcements to protect yourself? How will you guard your castle? How will you be able to look out?

The enemy loves it when we have no clue how he keeps getting inside. He likes naïve princesses with unguarded castles. He revels when we have no windows to see how he keeps getting in. He wins when we're blind to his ways.

Without vision, the Bible says we perish (Proverbs 29:18). Without windows, we leave our castles unguarded and susceptible to invasion. When we take the time to figure out the enemy's plot and protect our weaknesses, however, we can install security in place to defend our castles from further attacks.

WHAT IS THE LOOKOUT PLAN FOR YOUR CASTLE?

I'm not a fan of focusing on the past. Lot's wife taught me that lesson. She glanced behind her at Sodom even though the angel warned her, "Do not look back!" She loved her lifestyle and didn't want to leave. Her heart longed for her past. We all know how that worked out.

#saltywife #shouldhavelistened

Looking Back to Look Out

But there are times when it's important to look back. And one of those times is when we need to study the strategy of the enemy so we can guard our future. In other words, we don't look back to go back, we look back to look out.

I'm a *Law and Order* junkie. When Detectives Stabler and Benson are trying to nail a suspect, they may do a stakeout or launch a surveillance plan. They'll observe the subject in order to figure out his agenda. Their motive is simple: to arrest the suspect and stop him from committing any more crimes.

I also love the drama of *Chicago Fire*. When investigators look at fire remains, they study the destruction to determine how the fire started. Whether it was due to arson, faulty wiring, an appliance malfunction, or an explosion, they try to figure out ways to prevent another fire from happening in the future. Studying the evidence helps them prevent future destruction and know what not to do next time.

That's what we're going to do. We're going to be detectives and investigators. We're going to launch a surveillance plan to stop the enemy from committing any more crimes against us. We'll also study the evidence of our past emotional fires so we can prevent them from happening again.

Our investigative tools are windows. Windows give us an access point, a way to survey the enemy's plans in order to shut him down. Studying the evidence will help us prevent future demolition in our own castles.

Especially if we've ever said anything like:

- I didn't see that coming!
- We have the same fight almost every week.

- He knows just how to push my buttons!
- I keep attracting the same type of men over and over again. Men who take advantage of me. What's wrong with me?
- I've forgiven him so many times, but he never changes.
- I keep repeating the same mistakes over and over. What am I doing wrong?

HEAR HIM ROAR

The Bible compares Satan to a roaring lion. "Be alert and of sober mind. Your enemy the devil prowls around like a roaring lion looking for someone to devour (1 Peter 5:8)."

Lions are opportunists. So is Satan. He waits for an opportune time. He'll leave you alone when you're strong. But he's patient. He stalks you and waits to strike when you're alone, vulnerable, and not paying attention.

I did a little research on lions and was surprised to learn that they're not very fast. In fact, lions can only sprint at top speed in short bursts of approximately 300-400 meters before they run out of steam. What's even more surprising is that most of their prey can easily outrun them. Even so, they are able to dominate because:

- They're masters at hiding.
- They're phenomenally patient.
- They observe and stalk their prey during the day.
- They look for the weak, young, hurt, or injured—the one who is alone.
- Their attacks are most successful at night, under the cover of darkness.

- They hunt in groups, circling their prey until one of the lions is close enough to pounce. They may use an ambush technique. One lion lies in wait while another, on the other side, roars and causes the prey to run straight into the trap of the other lion.
- They're predators and opportunists.
- They don't roar until the prey is near enough to conquer.

It's easy to be alert and sober minded when you know the enemy is near, but lions don't roar while they're stalking their prey. Otherwise, they'd scare them away. They only roar when their prey is so close that there's no way for them to escape. If you're expecting an alarm to sound, by the time you hear it, it's too late.

The enemy will use any offense he can to trip you up. He'll study you to know where you're most vulnerable. That's why it's so important to identify your weaknesses. When you know where the enemy most often sneaks in, you can put guards in place to protect yourself.

THE DEVIL HAS A KEY

My friend Laura came home one morning and noticed a large wine spill on her carpet. "It freaked me out because my husband was at work, so it couldn't have been him. Even though there was no sign of a break in, someone had been in my apartment."

Startled, Laura ran to the office to see if one of the maintenance men had been in. No one had. Later that day, she found one of her ex-boyfriend's ball caps on her husband's tennis shoes. That's when it hit her. Her ex still had a key to her apartment, and he was trying to scare her and intimidate her husband.

Like Laura's ex, the devil loves to intimidate you. You may not know he's broken in until you notice something wrong. Laura changed her locks. She learned the hard way: not all invasions are done at gunpoint. Some devils have a key.

HOW ELSE DOES HE GET IN?

"I can't believe it happened again," said Terri. "I swore I'd never fall for another man who treated me this way again. I should have known better."

Sound familiar? Where you've been attacked on a repeated basis is your best clue about where the enemy is gaining access. It's the place where you're caught off guard. Where you're unprotected. I call these castle cracks. They're places where you trust too much. Where you have no boundaries or feel unworthy. When you discover the point of entry, however, you can seal it shut and declare, "Game over!"

Every crack in your foundation began with a lie—a lie you embraced as truth. It's a lie so embedded, you may not realize it's there. It's become engrained in your thought patterns and influences your behavior, reactions, and responses as if you were on autopilot. The lie came first, but it's buried so deep, all you notice now is the crack in your foundation.

One of the lies that I believed from an early age is that I didn't deserve what I really wanted. The lie made it into my castle by the way of a seven-dollar dime-store dress.

My parents grew up in the depression. As a result, they spent money with extreme caution. When I was about eight years old,

I went to the local five-and-dime with my mother. (For those of you too young to know what a five and dime is, it's like a discount supercenter.) I saw a mustard colored dress that I wanted. I didn't like the color, and it wasn't the prettiest dress I'd seen, but I knew my mom wouldn't buy me a dress at one of the boutiques where my friends shopped. They were too expensive, but this dress was only seven dollars. I asked my mom to buy it for me. When she said no, I was devastated. I pitched such a fit that she relented.

I went home with a new dress, but that day a crack formed in the foundation of my castle. A poverty mentality spread like wildfire into every area of my life and convinced me that I didn't deserve what I wanted. Then the lie dug its roots deeper and convinced me: *You'll have to beg to get something inferior.* When I got old enough to date, the roots that had grown deep in my belief system caused me to compromise in relationships. Why would a guy I liked be interested in me? The great catches were for the cuter and more popular girls. I'd have to settle for anyone who'd look my way. I may not have really liked him, but having someone was better than having no one at all.

CATASTROPHIC CASTLE CRACKS

The most damaging castle cracks form at an early age. Over time, all of these cracks cause bitterness to build and deteriorate the foundation of your castle. That's why it's important that you find out how the enemy keeps getting in. Ignorance is not bliss. Ignorance makes you defenseless. As you read the list below and the examples that follow, you may think of other dysfunctional behaviors you've adopted in relationships or lies you've believed. If so, jot them in the margin.

- We don't trust our instincts.
- We have to be right and prove ourselves.
- We must be perfect.
- We think it's our fault.
- We have no boundaries.
- We think crazy is normal.
- We overlook red flags.
- We're too trusting.
- We help too much.
- We feel unworthy.

Now, let's examine how those cracks might form and how they continue to grow and influence our behavior later in life. Identifying the cracks will help us uncover the lies we've believed. In the following chapter, we'll begin the work of replacing the lies with God's truth.

We Don't Trust our Instincts
"When I met Daniel, sparks flew like crazy. We had this instant connection," said Jen. "We met on Match, and after our first date we talked on the phone for hours almost every day. I'd finally met my soul mate. Since he and his ex-wife had two children together, I wasn't concerned that he still had contact with her. But then I noticed little things, like he'd stay at her house for dinner when he dropped the kids off or went shopping with her for back-to-school clothes. He said it was to provide stability for the children. At one point I wondered if they were hooking up, but I wrote it off as my

Every **crack** in your foundation **began** as a lie—a lie you embraced as truth.

imagination. We were in love, and I couldn't imagine that he'd lie to me. Turns out, they'd been sleeping together the whole time we'd been dating. I should have paid attention to my gut."

We Have to be Right and Prove Ourselves

"I grew up with an older brother who always got away with everything," said Hollye. "One time he accidentally broke a window playing baseball outside. Guess who got blamed? I had to stand in the corner for what seemed like hours. The more I argued, the more my mom accused me of lying and added minutes to my time-out. Living in my brother's shadow made me feel invisible. Like no one ever listened to me. Maybe that's why I was so good at debate in high school. The truth was, I wasn't that interested in the topics we argued. I wanted to win to prove my worth. Now, even in my marriage, I have this insatiable need to be right. My husband and I fight over trivial things like which is the fastest way to the grocery store or the best way to load the dishwasher. It's ridiculous."

We Must be Perfect

"I'm a smart girl," said Janie. "I have wonderful, amazing, beautiful kids, and a great career that is very financially rewarding. But I feel empty. I think I have always felt this way. As long as I can remember, I've lived most of my life operating out of shame. I got pregnant a month shy of sixteen and terminated the pregnancy. Obviously, my parents were involved. It "got fixed," and it has never been spoken of again. To this day (I'm forty-six now) that shame kept me from trying things I wanted to do, like try out for cheerleader or rush at college. I was afraid if people knew about what I did, they'd think I was a horrible person, since I was such an embarrassment to my parents."

Amber's lie started much younger. "When I was about eight years old, I was watching my mom finish a dress in her sewing room. She asked me to look in her sewing kit and hand her a bobbin. I didn't know what it was, but was too afraid to ask. When I handed her a presser foot instead, she yelled at me and said, 'Don't you know what a bobbin is?' I felt so stupid and embarrassed. That's when I learned that in order to be accepted, I needed to be perfect. Ever since then, I've strived to find out things for myself so I would never be humiliated like that again. If anyone, especially my husband or boss, ever questions me, I get easily triggered and angry."

We Think it's our Fault

"I'm always the one to apologize," said Jenny. "For no reason at all. I can't stand to think someone might be upset with me. If someone doesn't smile at me at work, I think I must have done something wrong. It never occurs to me that maybe they're focused on a project or didn't even see me. I just assume somehow I've made them mad."

Jenny was sexually abused by her uncle from the time she was five years old. She was too young to understand that his moral failure was not a reflection of her worth. Instead, she internalized the shame and embraced several lies: *I'm not worthy. I'm guilty. No one will ever love me. If something goes wrong, I have to fix it. If I can't fix it, it's my fault.*

Jenny was married for twenty-four years. "The entire time we were married, he was having an affair with one of the secretaries at our church. I can't believe I stayed so long. Somehow I thought if I could make him happier, be a better wife, he wouldn't be unfaithful."

We Have No Boundaries

"I never saw my parents argue or fight," said Denise. "If my dad made my mom mad, I never knew it. I got the impression that submission meant I had to agree with everything my husband said. I felt like a horrible wife because there were lots of things I didn't agree with Jason about. But since I thought God hated any type of marital conflict, I stuffed my frustration inside and pretended everything was okay. Eventually I got so angry and depressed I could hardly function."

Women who haven't learned how to set boundaries have believed all kinds of lies: *I should agree and make others happy. Standing up for myself is selfish. A good wife always covers her husband's faults.* Maybe she's misinterpreted scripture or was taught that it was ungodly to disagree with her partner or spouse. That was the case with LaRonda.

"He was the cruelest man I've ever known," said LaRonda, "but I kept thinking I must have deserved it. Somehow it was my fault. If only I was nicer and prayed more, things would change. I can't believe I was so stupid."

We Think Crazy is Normal

"Is there a magnet on my head?" Tracy sighed. "Why do I always pick out the crazy ones?"

Tracy's mother was an alcoholic who was divorced three times by the time Tracy was twelve. "I never remember a time when my mom wasn't fighting with one of her husbands. It was hard to get my homework done or to sleep at night because of all the arguing. My teachers thought I was slow. I wasn't stupid. I was sleep deprived."

When we've grown up with constant arguing, we may embrace

it as a normal part of a relationship. We're desensitized to the chaos. If we've never learned healthy conflict resolution skills, we're unprepared to function in a peaceful relationship. If all we've ever witnessed is verbal abuse (yes, verbal abuse is abuse) as painful as it is, peace feels foreign. Chaos is normal. We tolerate discord, thinking there's no better way.

It's true that people who love each other disagree. But to someone who was raised in a verbally abusive environment, disagreements escalate into explosive arguments, name calling, and sarcasm. That was the case with Tracy. As a result, her tolerance for conflict was high. All she'd ever known was drama. To her it was normal. Without the ability to filter out unacceptable behavior, Tracy was oblivious to the fact that she was drawn to abusive men.

We Overlook Red Flags

"I expected Jackson to be as caring and as sensitive as I am," said Shaye. "That's one of the qualities he appreciated so much about me. He used to go on and on about how considerate I was. It was kind of flattering, and I guess I assumed it was important to him too, even though he seemed to have a temper. I overlooked his angry outbursts when we were dating. I chalked it up to the stress he felt about being a single dad and thought after we got married, things would be better because I'd be around to help. But after the honeymoon, things got worse overnight. I shouldn't have minimized the issues with his temper. I feel like I'm always walking around on egg shells."

When we project our own values on others and assume they have the same standards as we do, we're setting ourselves up for disappointment. Having unmet expectations is one of the biggest bitterness traps. Pay attention to red flags. Problems that we notice in the beginning of a relationship are often magnified after marriage.

We're Too Trusting

"I met my husband at church," said Kendra. "He seemed like a dream come true and said all the right things. I gave him a pass because he was a deacon. That title carried a lot of weight, and I assumed he was a godly man. But the day we got married, I had this creepy feeling walking down the aisle."

Isn't love supposed to trust? Yes, but with both eyes wide open. We don't give our trust away. It must first be earned. Don't assume that just because a guy attends church, he loves the Lord. Pay attention to his actions. They don't lie. If a man loves God, it will show in the way he treats you and others. Judas is a great example. He was close *to* Jesus, but he wasn't close *with* Jesus. In the same manner, a man can be *in* church but *out* of relationship.

We Help Too Much

It's easy to see how women are prone to destructive romantic relationships when they've grown up in dysfunctional families. But that wasn't the case with Morgan. "My childhood and home life were wonderful," said Morgan. "I grew up in a loving Christian home. My parents are still married, and my father always made me feel secure. I've never doubted his love for me.

"When I was in junior high and high school, our family went on several mission trips. It was horrible seeing the living conditions in the places we visited. The people there didn't do anything to deserve the poverty that surrounded them. I felt so sorry for them, but that all washed away when I saw their faces. They radiated gratitude.

That's when I fell in love with serving people in desperate need. And maybe that's when I assumed that everyone in difficult situations wants to get better."

Morgan's servant heart and happy home life created some unrealistic expectations. Since her father was kind and honest, she assumed all men were. And since her missionary experiences helping those less fortunate was pleasant and rewarding, she expected the same results in a romantic relationship. When problems surfaced, she assumed her guy would want to get better and would be glad to accept her help.

"When I met my first husband, it never occurred to me that he might lie about drinking or being with other women. He assured me in great detail of his faithfulness, but he went to the lake a lot with his buddies. When I noticed pictures of him on Facebook with several girls in bikinis, he promised they were just friends. I felt incredibly judgmental for not believing him.

"A few months after we started dating, his drinking got out of control. He was a belligerent angry drunk, calling me names and blaming me for everything under the sun. As horrific as it was, when he sobered up, he always promised to change. It worked every time. I'm a sucker for someone who wants to change. Plus, I felt guilty that I'd had such a great upbringing and his had been terrible. His parents divorced when he was ten, and he hadn't seen his father since. I felt obligated to help him change.

"Despite all the warning signs, I married him. But his drinking got worse, and I suspected that he was unfaithful. I kept thinking if I just were kinder and tried harder to help him, he would change."

Maybe you're reading this and thinking, *I wouldn't put up with that. I'd be gone in a heartbeat.* Then this is not your castle crack.

The enemy won't waste his time trying to wiggle his way into your castle with a sad sob story. But for those with a bent toward the gift of mercy, it's easy for their compassion to be misguided. They may think their love and impact are measured by the amount they try to help. They may believe other lies like: *If you really cared, you wouldn't give up. You're not supposed to judge. They need you. Who will help them if you don't? They won't make it if you leave. They promised to change. Why don't you believe them?* For women who suffer from this castle crack, it's hard for them to let go.

We Feel Unworthy

Growing up as an energetic chatty young girl, I must have driven my dad crazy. I pestered him with a million questions. With lots and lots of stories. If I heard it once, I heard it a thousand times. After taking a long puff of his Swisher Sweet cigar, a cloud of smoke and frustration would billow out together. "Chrissie, hurry up! Get to the point. You talk too much."

My father didn't mean to discourage me, but the enemy of my soul did. He wanted to destroy my confidence.

I can just imagine his strategy: *Hmmm. A girl who thinks she has a voice? I'd better put a stop to that.* And who better to use to squash my heart than someone I loved—my father.

When my dad told me I talked too much, I started to believe him. And the enemy added some flavorful accusations to my father's impatience. Accusations like:

- *You have nothing important to say.*
- *You'd better keep your mouth shut.*
- *Nobody wants to hear your opinion because you're unworthy and insignificant.*

By the time I was in junior high, the energetic chatty girl was quiet. Reserved. Timid. Insecure. For a while at least, it looked like I was defeated. I learned to shut up before I ever had a chance to speak up.

The scoundrel starts with lies that begin at an early age. He knows that if he can convince us when we're young that we're worthless, we'll carry those thoughts into adulthood and into our relationships. Once the lies are embedded in our thoughts, we accept them as truth. Satan's aim is to make us weak and vulnerable and strangle us in bitterness.

We'll feel comfortable with insults because they're familiar to us. They don't just live on the lips of people we love; they live in our head.

For a while the enemy may win. But once we unravel his plan, the tables turn! I'm glad I'm onto him now. Once I figured out his strategy, I was able to install security in place to guard my castle. Now, the energetic chatty ~~young~~ girl is back. But this time…

I'm older and wiser.

I'm strong and free.

And I want you to be free, too!

Look Over the Castle Cracks Again

Which ones did you identify with the most? I pray that your eyes were opened in a new way. I hope that seeing how the devil strategically deceived you filled you with fury. Only this time, instead of your anger being aimed at yourself or others, now you can aim your wrath in the right direction—at that evil trickster. It's time to declare war! In the next chapter we'll look at the doors in our castle and ensure that they're equipped to keep toxic thoughts out. It's time to demolish the lies and deceit that permitted the cracks in the first place.

PONDER AND PRACTICE

1. How do the characteristics of lions give you more insight into Satan's strategy to devour you?
2. Which of the castle cracks did you identify with most?
3. What other lies has the devil tried to convince you of?

- 8 -

Self-Talk Matters

DID YOUR PARENTS EVER TELL you to watch your mouth? As a young girl, whenever I complained, cried, or criticized, my mother's voice rose a few octaves as she warned, "Christine, don't give me any lip! You'd *better* watch your mouth!"

I knew it was time to shape up when she used my full name.

My mom wasn't a Bible student, but if she had been, she'd have realized she was teaching me a spiritual principle. James talks about how a giant ship is steered by a tiny rudder (James 3:4-5). In the same way, our entire palace is controlled by one of the tiniest members of our body—our tongue.

Before a word is formed on our tongue, it's first a thought on our mind. Believe it or not, we get to choose what thoughts we allow ourselves to think about. You've no doubt heard the saying, *you are what you eat*. The same is true with your thoughts: you are what you think.

Your mind is like the door to your castle. Only you can decide what thoughts or meditations you allow inside. You also decide what meditations are *not* allowed to come in. Before we go on, I'd like to clarify a common misconception. Meditation involves much more than just our thoughts. In fact, the word *meditate* in the Hebrew means *to mutter*. Before a mutter is formed on your lips, it is first conceived as a thought. Thoughts come first, but the mouth speaks what the heart is full of (Luke 6:45).

When negative thoughts try to invade our castle and influence our emotions, we have the responsibility to kick them out. If a robber rang your doorbell and asked if he could come in and steal all of your valuables, you'd slam the door in his face, bolt it shut, and call 911. And yet when harmful thoughts try to rob our valuable peace, we often open the door and welcome them in. We may even offer them coffee and say, "Sit down for a while and let's talk."

I have a speakeasy on the front door of my house—a small-latched opening that allows me to talk to a person ringing the bell without opening the door. It's very useful because I can keep the door shut and locked while I decide if I want to allow the person the opportunity to come in. If it's my neighbor asking to borrow a ladder, I'll open the door. If it's a solicitor trying to sell magazines or pest control services, I'll probably tell them I'm not interested and close the speakeasy. I get to choose who I invite into my home. Just because someone rings the doorbell doesn't obligate me to welcome them inside.

That's the way we should deal with our thoughts. Just because a thought rings the doorbell of our castle doesn't obligate us to entertain it. We've got to learn to stop entertaining destructive thoughts. If we don't discipline our mind, our thoughts grow over time and create self-inflicted strongholds that hold us in bondage.

Satan's battleground is your mind. His brand of deception combines a lethal lie with a dash of truth. That way, a lie doesn't really sound like a lie. A lure of self-pity seems reasonable. The bait of bitterness seems justified. He makes pride seem like confidence and insecurity seem like humility. The list goes on. He twists and tweaks the truth, but if he can penetrate your brain, he can pollute your thought life. Refusing to consider thoughts that contradict what God's word says about you or your situation is what the Bible calls taking thoughts captive.

According to 2 Corinthians 10:5, we should demolish arguments and every pretension that sets itself up against the knowledge of God, and we should take captive every thought to make it obedient to Christ. Other versions of the Bible use a variety of terms to describe the arguments and pretensions that camouflage as logical thoughts: proud obstacles, vain imaginations, lofty opinions, arrogant speculations and reasonings.

Taking these thoughts captive is only part of the instruction this verse gives us. The second part of this directive is to make the thought obey Christ. In other words, we can't just deny or erase the thought. We have to replace the thought. And this takes some intentional and dedicated practice.

BITE YOUR TONGUE

Jana came in for a coaching session one afternoon. Upset and frustrated about a recent breakup, she complained. "I'm such a wreck. I thought everything was going great, but then out of the blue, Jason called it off. Said he's not ready for a commitment. It's not like I haven't heard those words before. I'm sure it's code for he's found someone sexier or smarter or both. I just need to face the facts—no guy is ever going to want me. I'm not enough."

I stopped her right there. Jana thought she was telling me the facts. In reality, she started off by reporting her circumstances, but when she allowed her emotions to influence her thoughts, she added her own conclusion and spoke a negative confession over herself. She didn't realize the power of her words.

Sometimes women give the devil too much credit for the things that go wrong in their lives, when in reality, their negative circumstances are the result of their own thoughts that give birth to destructive words. They open their castle door to the enemy when they don't take control of their mouth.

The enemy only has access to our life by our thoughts. When we don't take those thoughts captive, they grow into emotions and, over time, those emotions convert into words.

There's a huge difference between facts and truth. Let me explain. Facts are what we can see in our present reality. Truth is what God says, whether it's something we experience or not.

We build our castles with our words. Brick by brick, word by word, we build the foundation of our world with the power of our tongue. That's why we need to be careful what we declare. Proverbs 18:21 (NLT) says, "The tongue can bring death or life; those who love to talk will reap the consequences."

The creation story in Genesis tells us that God created light when all He saw was darkness. He didn't say what He saw. He declared what He *wanted* to see. He didn't report the facts and say, "Wow, Jesus, it sure is dark in our universe. I wonder how long we'll have to stumble around. Maybe someday things will get better." No! He didn't focus on what He saw. Instead, He declared what He wanted to see: "Let there be light!" (Genesis 1:3).

Notice that God didn't address the darkness. He didn't speak to the situation. He spoke the solution.

God created the world by the power of His spoken word

released into the atmosphere. And guess what? Because you're created in His image, you have authority to create with your own words. Your words can be used to bless or curse yourself or others. If your tongue is perverse, you'll fall into trouble (Proverbs 17:20). On the other hand, when you guard your words, you'll preserve your life (Proverbs 13:3).

As a daughter of the King, you've been given incredible authority. Resist the urge to report what your present circumstances reveal. Instead, speak and release God's truth. For example, in Jana's situation, when she said, "I just need to face the facts—no guy is ever going to want me. I'm not enough," she allowed her thoughts and words to agree with the accusations of the enemy. As a result, she often felt discouraged and rejected. When she recognized the mirage of Satan's deception, she decided to use her mouth to agree with God's truth. Now when those lies tempt her, she demolishes his arguments by taking those thoughts captive and making them agree with God's truth. Today her new truth fills her with courage and confidence as she declares, "I am loved and wonderfully made. I am cherished and chosen by Him. And as I delight myself in Him, He will grant me the desires of my heart."

When you align your thoughts with truth, you rule and reign over the darkness in your life. Just like God spoke to create light, He gave you the authority to create light in your own earthly kingdom.

The trouble many of us have is that when we don't see the immediate physical manifestation, we feel like we're lying to ourselves. We get impatient or give up because we think it doesn't work.

Our words, however, are like seeds. You don't plant a seed into the ground and expect a bouquet of flowers to pop up. When you click the Buy Now button on Amazon, you don't see a package in your mailbox or on your door step for a couple of days. You didn't click the button and think, *Where's my package? I guess it didn't work. I need to get a refund.* That would be ridiculous. You understand that it takes time for delivery. When the pregnancy test displays a positive result, you don't expect a baby for another nine months. Some things take time to manifest.

If you struggle with doubt that your words aren't working, don't give up hope. When results take time, remember that faith is the evidence of things not yet seen (Hebrews 11:1). You aren't lying when you declare God's truth. You're using your tongue to create life.

Stating the obvious takes no faith. It takes faith to declare what you cannot yet see. So stop declaring what you see now. If you're resolved to stay in your marriage despite its disappointments or difficulties (please know I'm not talking about a destructive marriage; no woman should endure an abusive marriage) remember, your contentment doesn't depend entirely on your spouse. Stop agreeing with the enemy and saying things like, "My life is a mess. I guess I'm just stuck with this misery." Why not use your tongue to declare something good and create life?

Your peace and satisfaction with life can return if you make a commitment to redirect your thoughts. Instead declare God's truth over your life: "God's grace is sufficient for me. The joy of the Lord is my strength. May the God of hope fill me with all joy and peace as I trust in him, so that I may overflow with hope by the power of the Holy Spirit."

If you're single, don't say things like, "All the good men are taken. I'll never find a husband. All men are lying snakes anyway." If you want to be married someday, agree with God's truth about your future. "As I delight myself in the Lord, He will grant me the desire of my heart. He knows my heart better than I do. I believe if it's His will for me to be married, I won't have to settle. He'll send me a God-fearing husband, a man who will cherish me and love me like he loves his own body. And if it's His will for me to be single, I trust that He'll help me remain content."

Over the next several months, Jana practiced truth statements. She bit her tongue and instead of declaring what she saw, she spoke God's truth over herself. As she did, her confidence increased. Her countenance changed. Ladies, truth changes you from the inside out. People will notice the difference. Because she saw herself through a different lens, Jana eventually quit attracting men who weren't serious about relationships. And guess what? She's now in a healthy relationship and engaged to be married.

It doesn't take faith to report our circumstances. It takes faith to redirect them. Our lives can experience dramatic changes when we bite our tongues and make our words agree with God's truth.

PRAY THE ANSWER

In Mark 4, after a long day of ministry, Jesus said to his disciples, "Let us go over to the other side." They all got in the boat, and Jesus feel asleep in the stern. When a furious squall sent waves over the side, the disciples ran to the bottom of the ship and woke Jesus up. "Don't you care that we're going to die?" they yelled.

My takeaway from this story is that it was Jesus' idea to go to the other side. That alone should have given the disciples confidence that everything would be okay. It's so easy to read this story and think of how I would have handled it. But I wasn't there. Waves on

A complaining *tongue* strips prayer of its *power.*

a page can't make me afraid. It's only when the darkness of night surrounds me and I feel the water up my nostrils that my faith is tested to the core.

In my own life, I've often felt led by the Lord to go this way or that way. And when waves threatened to capsize my life, my faith looked just like the disciples' faith. Only my prayer wouldn't have been a one-liner. It would have been an entire paragraph. It would have sounded something like, "Dear Jesus, this storm is huge. I've never seen anything like it. My boat is about to capsize, and there's no coast guard. I'm freaking out. I have no life boat. I'm so frightened and sure this storm is going to kill me. Please *help* me, in Jesus' name. Amen."

And all the while, Jesus wouldn't be worried about my problem. He'd lift his sleepy head off of his pillow and speak to the storm as if he were swatting a fly. "Quiet, be still."

Then he'd look at me and say, "Why were you so afraid? Do you *still* have no faith?"

This story makes it clear. When we give fearful thoughts power, they evolve into fearful declarations. Our words have power, but we don't have to tell God about our problems. He already knows. We don't have to give him a detailed play-by-play of everything that's wrong. When Jesus opened his mouth, he didn't speak *about* the storm; he spoke *to* the storm. He used his words to change his reality. He spoke with power and authority what he wanted to see.

Quiet, be still.

I hope you'll try it next time you're afraid. When the enemy whispers lies like, you're not going to make it. You're not good enough. You don't have what it takes. You're last in line. No man will want you because you have too many kids. No man will want you because you can't have kids. You're too old. Too silly. Too smart. Too whatever.

Roll over and swat at the lying deceiver—quiet, be still!

DOES GOD HEAR OUR PRAYERS?

If I asked the question, "Does God hear our prayers?" I bet you'd say, "Absolutely!" But what about this question: Does God hear our complaints?

I believe He does. In fact, I'd venture to say that grumbling is a very popular form of prayer. When the Israelites left the bondage of Egypt, they prayed daily, but their prayers were idle words and bitter complaints.

"But now we have lost our appetite; we never see anything but this manna!" (Numbers 11:6). "If only we had died in Egypt! Or in this wilderness! Why is the Lord bringing us to this land only to let us fall by the sword?" (Number 14:2-3).

Have you ever muttered prayers like that? *I was better off back there! Why, God, why? My husband never listens. I'm better off alone.* Friends, we have to watch our mouths. The tongue is like a battery. Positive and negative energy cancel each other out. Likewise, a complaining tongue strips prayer of its power.

God had heard enough of the Israelites' complaints, and he said this to Moses: "How long will this wicked community grumble against me? I have heard the complaints of these grumbling Israelites. So tell them, 'As surely as I live, declares the Lord, I will do to you the very things I heard you say'" (Numbers 14:28).

I wonder if my father had read this story in the Bible. When I was little, he used to tell me, "Christine, you'd better be quiet or

Self-Talk Matters

I'm gonna give you what you're asking for!" Dad had had enough! So had God. Except for Joshua and Caleb, every one of the Israelites who crossed the Red Sea died in the desert. Their prayers were answered. They got what they prayed for.

The children of Israel taught us a powerful truth. Our fear-filled thoughts give birth to words spoken in fear and make our words spoken in faith of no effect. Frequent idle words, curses, and complaints turn our hearts away from truth. It's a gradual process that leads to destruction and emotional bankruptcy.

COMPLAINING CANCELS OUT WORDS OF FAITH

Tiffany reached for a Kleenex. "I've been praying every day for Alex and me to get along." She crossed her arms and sighed. "Things go well for a while, but when something irritates him, he clams up. He says he needs time to process his thoughts, but it drives me crazy. I want to resolve it right then and there. I can't take it anymore. I told him I'd rather have him yell at me than not tell me what he's thinking."

Tiffany had a good habit of praying every day for her relationship, but, when she got frustrated, she used her words to create something she really didn't want. Instead of saying what she wanted to see, she said what she saw. She allowed her thoughts of frustration to control her mouth instead of allowing her faith to take over. As a result, she aggravated Alex, and his calm demeanor turned angry.

One day while listening to *Enjoying Everyday Life*, Joyce Meyer mentioned on her program, "If you're going to keep complaining about something, don't bother praying about it."

If you ever need a spiritual spanking, Joyce delivers!

Don't declare positive confessions in prayer and then turn around and complain. Words of fear cancel out words of faith. Elizabeth Elliot puts it this way. "Don't dig up in doubt what you planted in faith."

I want to challenge you: don't just speak what you see. News reporters do that. If you want to change your situation, it starts with your tongue. Your tongue is to your life what a steering wheel is to a car. You will go in the direction of your mouth (James 3:1-4). Your confession will change your direction. God gave you the authority to use your words to create your world. Your words change the atmosphere of your castle, so make them count.

OUR WORDS CREATE OUR WORLD

When we focus on our problems, we lose sight of God. When we focus on God, we lose sight of our problems. I experienced the gravity of this truth when I was pregnant with Garrett, my middle child. During my fourth month of pregnancy, my OB-GYN had alarming concerns. As she measured my fundal height, a look of worry spread across her face. "I think you may have intrauterine growth delay," she announced. "I need to you come back in two weeks for further testing."

I was shocked. I felt fine. *What could be wrong with my baby?*

Two weeks seemed like two years. When I went back, her suspicions were confirmed.

"Your baby isn't growing. He isn't receiving nutrition from the placenta. There's also something wrong with his heart, and I'm concerned about the possibility of Down syndrome."

I left Dr. Huff's office that day numb. Wandering into Hobby Lobby, I hoped that somehow decorating distractions would prove her wrong. After looking around for a bit, I left in a daze without making a purchase. Walking to my car, I heard a whistle from behind me.

Really? I thought to myself. *What kind of weirdo tries to hit on a pregnant lady?*

I glanced over my shoulder. It was David Thomas, one of the pastors from my church. "How are you, Christy?" He gave me a hug.

I fell apart in his arms. "I just left my doctor's office."

"What's wrong?"

As I sobbed, I said, "She told me I had a condition called intrauterine growth delay."

"Oh, my wife had that, too," he said with a shrug. "It's going to be all right. Doctors, you know…it's probably just CYA."

"CYA?" I asked. "What's that?"

"Cover Your…ahem…you know."

My eyebrows nearly touched my hairline.

"They told my wife and me the same thing. Of course we were devastated, but in time we realized that no matter what happened, we couldn't let the diagnosis steal our peace. You won't be able to endure your situation without it either!"

Pastor David said a short prayer over me right there in the Hobby Lobby parking lot. As he said good-bye, he paused. "Christy, just remember this. You have to renew your mind. When you think about your situation, be careful what thoughts you give permission to linger. Otherwise you'll lose the peace and strength you need to endure."

I got in my car and drove home, marveling that God put my pastor in my path to immediately defuse the enemy's tactics to steal my peace. I made a decision. I was going to trust God despite what my circumstances looked like.

During my next visit, Dr. Huff put me under the supervision of a perinatologist, an obstetrical subspecialist, to supervise the potential complications of my high-risk pregnancy.

Throughout the rest of my term, I saw other specialists, including a fetal cardiologist, who monitored Garrett's heart. While I considered their wisdom and caution, I resolved to align my thoughts and my words with God's truth. It wasn't easy, but I was encouraged by Pastor David's wisdom. I decided to rewrite the movie script that had been playing out in my mind.

When fear gripped me, I fought the enemy by using my mouth as a sword against him.

When I am afraid, I put my trust in God.

I will say of the Lord, He is my refuge and my fortress.

I will trust in the Lord with all my heart and lean not on my own understanding.

Despite the fact that Garrett didn't grow in utero, a confident peace consumed me. My circumstances hadn't changed, but because my mind was fixed on truth, anxiety and fear had less leverage to taunt me.

"I'm still concerned about heart defects," said Dr. Huff. "I'll have a pediatric cardiologist with me in the delivery room ready to perform any necessary heart surgery. If you can make it to thirty-seven weeks, however, at least your baby's lungs will be fully developed. That's one less thing we'll have to worry about. We can induce then."

Self-Talk Matters

Thirty-seven weeks came, and I was ready to have my baby. On Nov 5, 1992, Dr. Huff started my drip, but after several hours of labor, Garrett wasn't tolerating the contractions. "We'll have to do an emergency C-section," she said.

Like a sudden tsunami, my room flooded with doctors and nurses and machines. They wheeled me to the operating room. My mind fixed on truth as the anesthesia took effect.

I put my trust in God.

Garrett weighed in at a hefty three-and-a half pounds, but when the cardiologist performed the exam, he found no heart defects. "Other than a functional heart murmur that he should eventually outgrow, your baby boy is healthy."

A wave of relief washed over me. Garrett spent two-and-a half weeks in the neonatal unit to gain weight. When I brought him home, however, new challenges arose.

When Garrett was a baby and toddler, he fell several times and lost consciousness. Twice I picked up his limp body as his eyes rolled back into his head as if he were dead. Those were the scariest moments of my life. That's when I realized that the practice of choosing peace was not just for a season; it needed to be a lifetime habit.

Since it was unclear if he was having seizures, his pediatrician recommended that I take him to see a neurologist. "It may be a breath-holding spell—a response to a mild head trauma, but a neurologist can run some tests."

The tests, however, were inconclusive. Without witnessing an episode, he couldn't diagnose what was wrong. As a precaution, he gave me the option of putting Garrett on anti-seizure meds, but I opted not to. Again, I renewed my mind. With great determination,

I vowed to kick out any thoughts that didn't produce peace.

The challenge to think on whatsoever things are true, noble, right, pure, lovely and admirable (Philippians 4:8) strengthened me. Offending thoughts didn't belong in my castle. Instead I renewed my mind with God's truth. The last episode occurred when Garrett was four, and besides the car accident that occurred when he was five, he's been strong and healthy ever since. At the time of this writing, Garrett is twenty-six. My six-foot-tall musician is one of the greatest gifts God has ever given me, but what if I missed the joys of raising him because I focused on fear?

Maybe you read this story and said to yourself, *I tried that. I aligned my thoughts and my words with God's truth, but my circumstances didn't change. My husband still filed for divorce. My fiancé still cheated on me. My ex still tries to turn my children against me.*

Like you saw in my story, not everything changes overnight. And sometimes, the only change occurs on the inside. Our circumstances don't change, but *we* grow stronger. *We* find freedom.

God's word is not a promise that things outside of our castle will change. But it is a promise that the inside of our castle will be transformed. We are transformed when we renew our minds (Romans 12:2). Our situation may not change, but our serenity does. Instead of fear and dread, we enjoy peace and confidence. Our forecast may not change but our outlook does. Instead of insecurity and worry, we enjoy laughter and assurance that somehow everything will turn out for our good (Romans 8:28).

Who wants anxiety and dread? Who wants fear and torment? Who wants shame and sorrow? Even if nothing changes outside of our castle, on the inside we experience more peace and confidence. When we renew our minds, we experience an inner transformation.

SELF-TALK MATTERS

Anxiety, fear, shame and sorrow have a way of resurfacing well after a trial is over, but so does peace. So don't grow weary in well doing. And don't allow your mouth to get lazy by speaking idle words. Refuse to let your circumstances dictate your future. When your promise takes longer than you think it should, don't lose heart. Your due season is on its way (Galatians 6:9).

PONDER AND PRACTICE

1. Beside some of the following lofty opinions, what other vain imaginations or lies do you often hear others say?
    a. All men just want one thing.
    b. I can't help the way I am. I've always been this way.
    c. He'll never understand me.
    d. _____.
2. What idle words do you have a habit of saying?
3. How can you rephrase those words to align with God's truth and bring life?
4. Say the prayer below to ask God to help you watch your mouth.

Prayer: Lord, I want to honor You with my lips. Please help me take notice when I speak idle words that don't bring life. Help me to release words of faith that change me and encourage those around me. In Jesus' name. Amen.

- 9 -

Changing My Vision

ONE STORMY NIGHT WHEN MY daughter Brittany was five, I was reading a bedtime story to her and her friend who was spending the night. It was raining hard when a thunderous clap startled us. Lightning followed seconds later. I sensed the Lord tell me to stop and pray right then. Not at the end of the story, but right then. I closed the book for a moment and told the girls we were going to pray. "God, please protect our house from this lightning storm. May You put a hedge of protection around us."

After we finished praying, I continued the story and tucked them into bed. The next morning, my neighbor knocked on my door. "Can I use your phone," she asked. "Lightning struck our house last night, and all our phones and electrical appliances are fried."

Holding back shock, I walked her into the kitchen and handed her the phone.

She dialed a number to her insurance company. "Of course, they put me on hold," she said. Combing her fingers through her hair, she let out a chuckle. "Whenever my husband irritates me, I tell him, 'You keep that up and someday you're going to get struck by lightning.'"

Changing My Vision

Obviously, she didn't know the power of her words.

I know this is an exceptional example. Not all idle words are as extreme as my neighbor's. But her story is a powerful illustration to remind us about how important our words are. We shouldn't allow words to slip out of our mouths that we don't want to show up in our future. The Bible calls these idle words. They are empty, vain, or worthless.

Some idle words seem innocent.

That's just the way life is.

He only wants one thing.

Some idle words seem like a good way to let off steam.

He'll never listen.

Things will never get better.

I'd rather be alone.

Most of the time, we don't really mean these words. Spoken out of frustration, we don't want them to come to pass, but we're held accountable for the idle words we speak (Matthew 12:36).

Please don't think that I'm saying that all careless words result in chaos. Rather it's the disparaging words that we speak over and over again that change our belief system and cause damage.

Our faith is increased by what we hear, especially if the words come from our own lips. In other words, we can have faith for negative outcomes just as much as we have faith for positive outcomes. As soon as you recognize that you've allowed idle words to come out of your mouth, repent. Repent means to change. When you change your mind, you can change your words before they take root in your belief system.

If you're reading this and think that what I'm saying is far too extreme, let me say this. The devil is no fool. He knows that if you speak empty words and they manifest the very next day, you'll realize, "Oh, I better not say that!" He's a bit craftier than that. He'll let some time pass—just long enough that you fail to see the connection between what you see and what you said.

Bailey struggles with finances. She frequently complains that she's always broke.

Sharon's last three boyfriends were all unfaithful. She often says that all men are jerks.

Emily's husband is either working late or at the golf course. Emily whines that her husband never spends time with her.

Which came first? The consequence or the confession?

Even if our circumstances seem dismal, if we keep saying what we see, we'll keep seeing what we say.

Our thoughts may seem innocent, but they're progressive. Our thoughts turn into our feelings; our feelings influence our words; our words create our attitudes; and our attitudes become our actions and influence our vision. And when we don't have vision, a frightful thing happens—we forget how to see.

DON'T FORGET HOW TO SEE

"My mother-in-law is in the advanced stages of Alzheimer's Disease," the woman sitting across from me in the waiting room began. "After years of caring for her in our home, we finally had to put her in a nursing home."

She flipped through a health magazine. Her gaze never left the pages, but that didn't slow down her dialogue.

"She's broken so many bones because she keeps forgetting that she doesn't know how to walk. When she was with us, we had to constantly watch her. If we took our eyes off of her for a second, she would try to get out of bed and fall. She can't feed herself. She can't swallow—she's forgotten how. And now she's lost her eyesight. She's forgotten how to see."

"Forgotten how to see?" I'd never heard of such a thing. "How do you forget how to see?"

"The doctor says that there's nothing wrong with her vision, but the ability to see is controlled by the brain, not the eyes."

Soon, my name was called, and I said good-bye, but I couldn't get our conversation out of my mind. *The ability to see is controlled by the brain?*

Later that night I interrupted my husband's evening ritual. "John, did you know that we don't actually see with our eyes?"

Not even shifting his radar from *Law and Order* he muttered, "Yeah, the eyes only route information from the optic nerve. Visual perception actually occurs in the brain."

Occurs in the brain? How did he get so smart?

I don't remember learning how to see. It was instinct…effortless—like my reactions to life. In fact, I don't remember learning how to see my circumstances either. My view of life, my opinions and judgments, all soaked in as naturally as a sea sponge soaks in salt water. But after years of gradual contamination, my perception of life was weakened by false beliefs and failing emotions. My well-being depended on my perspective, but most of the time my focus was way off. So guess what? I grew miserable. And eventually, I forgot how to see.

When I was young, I depended on my relationships to make me happy. If my boyfriend called me every night, I'd be happy. If he paid more attention to me, I'd be happy. When he asked me to marry him, I could be happy. Too many ifs and whens.

My vision was blurred for years. I went through most of my life looking at my circumstances with faulty vision, all because my focus was wrong. It took me years before I figured out that Jesus saves and does Lasik.

Now I'm able to see beauty everywhere. I can perceive and distinguish things I was once oblivious to. My circumstances don't rule my emotions, and I'm no longer miserable.

How about you? Do circumstances dictate your happiness? Do relationship issues consume your thoughts or control your joy? When we live with discouragement for extended periods of time, we quit trying to evict it. It's easier to let it stay. It becomes familiar, and we get good at disguising it. *Miserable? No, I'm just tired today. Depressed? Oh, I'll be fine. It's nothing. Angry? Nah, I'm good.*

It's time to see things from a different viewpoint. There is more to life than what your physical eyes reveal. God has a promised land He wants to show you. But you have to change your focus and look through spiritual eyes in order to see it.

DON'T BE A GRASSHOPPER

The book of Exodus details the story of how God led his people out of Egyptian bondage. They'd been slaves for over 400 years, but God saw their misery and planned a rescue. He had a promised land for them. A land flowing with milk and honey. Or in modern day terms, a land flowing with coffee shops and cafes, with bakeries and boutiques. This promised land was everything they'd ever dreamed of.

In order to help them escape, God performed miracle after

miracle. Then, in an epic move to destroy their enemy, He parted the Red Sea while the Israelites crossed over the Jordan River on dry ground. The Egyptian military followed in hot pursuit, but as soon as God's people reached the shore, the sea swallowed up the entire army, chariots and all.

Maybe you've seen the scene in a movie. This grand deliverance should have been proof of how much God intended to honor His promise to them. But bondage has a way of keeping us bound long after we've been released. It's because captivity is first mental. Images stay in our heads. Unless we renew our minds, instead of finding freedom, we stay stuck.

God told the Israelites that He had an enormous gift to give them. His promise was a covenant contract. They'd finally have their own home. In preparation for the move, their leader, Moses, chose twelve spies and sent them on a journey to scope out the promised land.

After forty days, the twelve returned with some of the evidence of the land. Two men hauled a single cluster of grapes on a pole between them. Grapes the size of watermelons—that's some ginormous fruit. As they set the colossal cluster down, they told Moses, "We went into the land to which you sent us, and it does flow with milk and honey!" (Numbers 13:27).

You'd think this was good news. They all agreed that the land was everything God said it was. But there was a catch.

But.

But is a three-letter word that can destroy a promise. Ten of the spies came back dragging defeat and created an opposition. "But the people who live there are powerful (Numbers 13:28)." "We can't attack those people; they are stronger than we are

(Numbers 13:31)."

All agreed, but only two believed.

The rest forgot about the miracle of the Red Sea. They forgot about God's promise. Giants destroyed their vision. Instead, ten spies focused on their problem—giants. And their problem defeated them before they ever attempted to move.

Their final verdict is a startling reminder of the downward demise of disbelief: "We seemed like grasshoppers in our own eyes, and we looked the same to them" (Numbers 13:33). The ten spread a bad report among the people, so much that the entire camp wanted to kill Joshua and Caleb, the only two spies who came back with a good report. Only two had the capacity to trust the promise of God. Joshua and Caleb tried to convince the rest. "We should go up and take possession of the land, for we can certainly do it" (Numbers 13:30). But their faith was rivaled by doubt.

God wanted to take His people to the Promised Land, but their minds were still in Egypt. They were incapable of defeating the giants because they were not mentally positioned for victory. Focus changed their countenance. They saw themselves as grasshoppers.

Nowhere does this passage indicate that the giants called them grasshoppers. The giants didn't taunt them with a chant of *Na-na, na-na, boo-boo. Stick your head in doo doo.* The ten spies concluded all by themselves that they were insignificant, weak, and incapable. They first saw themselves as defeated. Then their evaluation of their capability became the lens through which the giants saw them.

Comparison is an ugly enemy. Instead of realizing they were

God's gladiators, they saw themselves as defeated in their minds' eye. They went in courageous and came out cowards.

If your mind is in misery and you move to a penthouse on Fifth Avenue, you'll be drawn right back to despair until you change your viewpoint. It doesn't matter what your address is; if your head is in the ghetto, you'll go back to the garbage.

We have to be careful what thoughts we allow to penetrate the walls of our castle. Thoughts are invisible enemies that cause tremendous destruction to our vision. The twelve spies all had the same experience. They all faced the same giants, and yet ten of them saw themselves as insignificant, incapable and defeated.

What was the difference in their perspective? It was vision, their capacity to see. The ten allowed their circumstances to convince them that God's promise was not good enough. Their faithlessness was the result of a lie.

My friend, how you see yourself becomes the lens through which others see you. How you see yourself is contagious. Your self-image and belief system are projected outward and often become the screen through which others view you.

Do you ever wonder why some don't treat you with respect? When you view yourself as a grasshopper, the principle of the promised land applies. The ten spies kept an entire nation in bondage because they gave a bad report. Their opinion of their capability contaminated their worth. How you view yourself is also responsible for your emotional health. Don't heap garbage on yourself with trash talk.

My dear sister, here's the truth: you'll never get beyond what you think of yourself. Every promise and every problem is stored as an image. You'll never go further into your promise than what you have seen in your mind. The other half of this truth is that you won't get through this life without facing your share of giants. In order to arrive at your promised land, you have to learn how to focus on God's promises. You'll never conquer your promised land by looking at your problem or seeing yourself as unworthy, insignificant or incapable. If you don't believe you're able, it doesn't matter what God says about you. Your own thinking will defeat you and disqualify you.

SLAY YOUR GIANTS

Take a moment and ask yourself: are the thoughts and images in your self-talk more focused on the problem or the promise?

Imagine that your giant is like a huge wolf balloon at the Macy's Day parade. The wolf taunts you with its evil eyes. But you've had enough. You take out your bow and shoot an arrow at it. It deflates and shrinks before your eyes, slithering to the ground until it's a lifeless pile of nothing. It appeared to have substance, but it was only full of air. Satan's lies are like that. Puffed up. Evil. Weightless. Nothing. Only when we inflate them do they have any authority to persecute us.

If the problem has been your focus, I have good news. Your lack of vision doesn't disqualify you. His power is perfected in your weakness. I've never met a successful woman who was devoid of flaws and failures. But every successful woman I've met has learned how to see beyond her problem and into her promised land. All it takes is a shift of your gaze. When you adjust your vision and imagine your promised land between your eyeballs, you'll be positioned to conquer your promised land in the physical realm.

You'll never get *beyond* what you *think* of yourself.

Battles are defeated in your mind before they're ever defeated in reality. The devil will still try to gnaw you down at every angle, but make up your mind that you're not quitting.

When you no longer see yourself as a grasshopper, you'll slay your giants. Keep your eyes fixed straight ahead on what the Lord has promised you. Trust His vision. I want you to remain unmovable when the enemy taunts and teases and says, "Na-na, na-na, boo-boo."

Friend, with vision you will conquer your promised land. The enemy will still do his best to convince you that you're nothing. That you're not able. But the truth is that you are powerful. You're gifted. You're valuable, significant, and able to do all things through Christ who strengthens you (Philippians 4:13).

Whose report will you believe? Where will you fix your eyes? What vision will you allow your eyes to focus on?

It's time to stop letting your circumstances contaminate your promise. It's time to be like Joshua and Caleb. They came back with a good report. (Sometimes I wish I could put a little feminine twist on this story and call our heroines Josephine and Cali—#strongwomen. But that would be wrong because it's the Bible.) But these heroes saw something different. Why? Because they calibrated their vision to agree with God's promise. They refused to let the negative influence of those around them talk them out of His plan.

There's a difference between a good report and a bad report. A bad report is an evil report—something that contradicts what God's Word says. When we allow words to come out of our mouths that disagree with God's truth and His promises, we are reciting an evil report.

The twelve spies all had the same promise. But only Joshua and Caleb chose to believe that God would fulfill it. You have a promise. What God has promised you may be different from the promise God gave your friend. But if it's a promise from God, no matter how impossible it looks in the natural, it *is* possible.

Joshua and Caleb had to wait forty years in the desert for their promise to manifest. But in the meantime, God was working. When you plant seeds, you may not see anything for a long time, but in the meantime, under the dirt, life is exploding. Those flowers didn't start growing when they emerged above the ground. They were growing long before. In the same way, God is developing your dream. You may not see the beauty of it yet, but don't grow weary in well doing.

In the meantime, resist the evil reports.

The virgin Mary did. Despite the fact that she was a single mom in a day and age when women were stoned for adultery, Mary believed God. When the angel told her she would conceive the Savior, Mary told the angel, "May your word to me be fulfilled" (Luke 1:38). When Joseph said he intended to divorce her quietly, she pondered the promise in her heart. When her circumstances looked bleak, she clung to truth. Mary refused to accept an evil report.

That's what Joshua did too.

SEE!

After forty years of wandering in the wilderness, everyone who left Egypt had died except for Joshua and Caleb. After the death of Moses, the Lord appointed Joshua to take the people into the promised land, and He told him this: "I will give you every place where you set your foot, as I promised Moses" (Joshua 1:3). "No one will be able to stand against you all the days of your life" (Joshua 1:5).

God gave Joshua an oath of victory, but with the covenant, there were a few commands. Four times in chapter one, the Lord tells Joshua, "Be strong and courageous." Whenever my parents repeated something more than once, it meant that instruction was super important. I needed to pay more attention. God's instructions are the same. The opposite of strong and courageous is weak and discouraged. God knew that if Joshua was weak and without courage, he'd move forward in defeat. He'd forfeit his inheritance.

Before the Israelites entered the Promise Land, the Lord visited Joshua and laid out the strategy for the battle of Jericho. In Joshua 6:2 the Lord says, "See! I have delivered Jericho into your hands, along with its king and its fighting men."

The first thing God said was, "See!"

Let me say this—nothing has happened yet.

Nothing.

But God wanted Joshua to be able to see the victory in the spirit realm before it occurred in the natural. If he couldn't see it in his mind, he'd never see it in time.

See comes from a Hebrew word that means: to look at, to perceive, to consider, to watch, to give attention to, to have vision and to gaze at. What we gaze at determines our direction. What we gaze at is the foundation of our victory.

Earlier, God told Joshua not to be discouraged several times. It's interesting to note that the word *discourage* comes from a Hebrew word that means *to turn your gaze away*.

Joshua could either gaze at God's promise and have courage or

Changing My Vision

turn his gaze away and end up discouraged.

In the same way, we either have vision, hope, and confidence in God's promise or we turn our gaze away and end up discouraged. When we're discouraged, we see ourselves as grasshoppers and never enter the place of promise God has for us. Furthermore, discouragement not only affects our emotional health; over time it impairs our physical health as well.

With the exception of Caleb, every other person who left Egypt with Joshua died in the desert. But Joshua remained strong even in his old age. At eighty-five years old, he made this statement: "I am still as strong today as the day Moses sent me out; I'm just as vigorous to go out to battle now as I was then" (Joshua 14:11). I want to say that when I'm in my golden years.

It takes vision to get the victory, and Joshua had it. He understood that every thought is stored as an image. If he wanted to see the victory, he had to change the mental picture in his mind. He had to change the reel.

In his book *The Healing Code,* Dr. Alex Loyd, writes, "… all memory is stored as pictures, and some of these pictures have non-truths or lies in them which, if left uncorrected, eventually result in emotional and/or physical disease."[13]

The good news is that you can change the pictures.

That's what Joshua did. He saw the victory in his imagination before the battle ever began. And so can you. By keeping your focus beyond your circumstances and on the promise God has given you, your confidence shifts into a covenant courage. It's time to stop letting your circumstances lie. Don't let them contaminate your promise. Govern your mouth with God's truth and watch. The words you speak today create your reality tomorrow.

CHOICE WORDS

If you want to change your life, you have to change your mouth. So often our prayers are just reporting the circumstances. Jesus never said to speak *about* the mountain. He said to speak *to* the mountain (Mark 11:23). Speak with the voice of truth and declare what you want to see in your future.

Joshua didn't pray, "Dear Lord, the city of Jericho is indestructible. Armed soldiers guard every inch of the wall. Our people are not well trained in battle, and our equipment is no match for their armory. Please help. I have no idea how to fight this battle."

Instead, he agreed with God's plan. How was he able to believe God against such great odds? Because for forty years he fixed his mind on God's truth that God would make good on his word. There was a promised land, and Joshua couldn't wait to get his eyes on it again. He didn't give up. He kept the vision before him. It strengthened him, not only spiritually, but physically as well. What if he had allowed the complaints of those around him to compromise his faith? Do you think his strength would have faded?

Joshua knew that God's truth is greater than the facts of what he could see in the physical realm. His prayer wasn't a petition. He already had the promise. He no longer needed to ask. Instead, his prayer was a simple and yet bold declaration of truth. "Shout! For the Lord has given you the city!" (Joshua 6:16).

LET YOUR WORDS BRING LIFE

The authority you have as a believer is first cultivated by your thoughts, groomed with vision and then released with your words.

Changing My Vision

Your vision and mouth work together to activate God's power in your life. In faith you speak and, as you do, your words influence your imagination. Your vision influences your expectations and faith rises up and starts the whole process all over again. In time, a miracle happens: your confidence and faith grow to new heights.

We've all been given a measure of faith, but often, without realizing it, we do more to diminish our faith than give it opportunity to grow. If you've ever said things like:

I'll always be alone.

All guys are jerks.

Men only want one thing. They're just looking to get laid.

You're activating your faith—only in reverse.

Proverbs 23:7 tells us that as we think in our heart, so shall we be. When we declare what we see now, we'll continue to get what we see now. Why? Because our hope is deflated when we complain. Remember the children of Israel? They wandered in the desert for forty years because they murmured and complained. They professed the problem and things never got better because they kept declaring the negative report.

I had a teacher in junior high who was often frustrated. Whenever she got irritated with our class, she'd throw her hands in the air and say, "My goodness! Y'all are going to drive me to my grave early." I once heard a sermon that gave some outstanding advice: If you can't add the phrase, *and that's just the way I want it*, after your statement, don't say it.

This advice gives brand new perspective to some of our negative confessions.

I'll always be alone. And that's just the way I want it. Ouch!

All guys are jerks. And that's just the way I want it. Not!

Men only want one thing. They're just looking to get laid. And that's just the way I want it. Doubtful.

Adding this addendum is a great way to measure truth. I'll admit. It takes faith to turn our tongue around. But when we use our mouth to promote blessings instead of provoke problems, we feel so much better. When we release blessings, the atmosphere shifts and our hope is elevated. Let's take a look at how some of these same statements would sound with a positive slant.

I may not have a partner now, but God has wonderful plans for me. And that's just the way I want it.

The world is full of decent men with honorable intentions. And that's just the way I want it.

How did it make you feel when you read the negative declarations? Upset, angry, discouraged? How did it made you feel when you read the positive declarations? Confident, hopeful, encouraged? I hope you see the difference. Using our mouth to speak hope and truth can not only influence the way we respond to others and create an atmosphere for our circumstances to change, it can also produce hope and confidence in us.

When we refrain from letting corrupt talk come out of our mouths, it gives grace to those who hear (Ephesians 4:29). And who hears our words the most but our own ears? Shouldn't we speak words that edify our own lives?

Gracious words are like a honeycomb. They bring sweetness to the soul and health to the body (Proverbs 16:24). This truth turned around would read like this: ungracious words are like vinegar. They bring sourness to the soul and sickness to the body. Who wants to risk having a sour soul or an illness?

Like a seed, the words you plant today create your reality

tomorrow. If you plant dandelions, don't expect roses to bloom. When you're careless with your words, you invite ruin. On the other hand, when you guard your mouth you preserve your life (Proverbs 13:3).

VISION CHANGES EVERYTHING

"When I found out about Mark's affair, I was devastated and angry," said Sheila. "We were both virgins when we married twenty-one years ago. I wasn't just angry with Mark, though. I was angry at God. My marriage wasn't supposed to be a statistic. We had a promise. When we first started dating, we sat on the back row at church. A traveling minister came to our service one day. He called us out and gave us a word. I guess he thought we were already married, but he said our marriage would be strong and that we'd have a powerful ministry. That's one of the reasons I married Mark. I always wanted to be a minister's wife. But now, even though Mark has sincerely repented, I feel like my dream is shattered."

Sheila and Mark were separated for a year when she came to see me. Sheila was miserable. She couldn't let go of the vision she'd clung to ever since the word was spoken over her and Mark. Through coaching, however, she realized she couldn't hang onto the bitterness and the vision. They didn't go together.

"If you keep the bitterness, you'll lose the vision," I told her. "But if you want the vision, you'll have to let go of the bitterness. You can't have both."

Sheila prayed that God would help her let go of her anger. "The enemy came to steal my marriage and my purpose, but I want it back," she said. "I don't want a divorce. I want to believe it's still possible."

I encouraged Sheila to get out her wedding album along with scriptures the Lord had given her and begin to renew her mind. "I needed pictures to go with the scriptures," said Sheila. "It helped me keep God's promises for my marriage alive."

Six months later, Sheila and Mark reconciled. Today, they lead a group in their church, ministering to other couples in marriage crisis. "God gave me the vision of our marriage before we were even married in order to give me endurance when it looked like it was over. Without vision, I'm sure we'd be divorced today."

Sheila made a good point. The Bible says that without vision we perish (Proverbs 29:18). We grow weary. We try to make things happen in our own strength and try to control the outcomes. We cast off restraint. You may have heard this scripture quoted like this: Without revelation we perish. I like this version better because the truth is that we all have vision. But we don't all have revelation.

In other words, we all have a picture or an image in our mind that propels us forward and influences our actions. Our emotional well-being, however, is the result of whether our vision was inspired by truth or the result of a lie we allowed ourselves to ponder.

The Hebrew word for vision is *chazown* and means a revelation or divine communication.

Joshua learned to keep the vision before him. When God laid out the battle plan for him, he didn't shrug it off as a silly dream. He refused to doubt. Instead he chose to believe. He focused his mind on what God said: "See, I've defeated Jericho!" Nothing had happened in the natural yet. The battle hadn't even started, but Joshua saw his victory before it happened. He won the battle in his mind first. That's what vision does. It makes faith manifest.

Where is your promised land? What does seeing your victory look like for you? Describe it in detail. Then begin to imagine it in faith. Use pictures, videos, sermons, or whatever else you need to stir your faith and inspire your imagination. Next, take it a step further and allow yourself to feel the victory. Describe it. What emotions are stirred within you?

This is not an exercise in fantasy. Fantasy is the devil's counterfeit for imagination. But God's gift to facilitate vision is imagination. When you align your vision with God's revelation for you, you refuse defeat and declare war.

God has victory in store for you. Winning occurs in your mind before it manifests physically. Spend time meditating and asking God for a revelation about your future. He wants to show you great and mighty things (Jeremiah 33:3). He wants you to see! Focus on the promise and watch what God will do. What you magnify in your thought life will multiply in your real life.

PONDER AND PRACTICE

1. Do you have scripture promises that you feel like were written just for you? That every time you hear them your heart leaps with hope? If so, what are they?
2. List any revelations, visions, or promises that God has given you about your future. (If you haven't heard from God in this way before, list the inner longings of your heart that you can't ignore. These are often clues to what God wants to do in your life.)
3. Describe what your future would look like if God's vision

for your life (or the desire of your heart that you can't ignore) came to pass.
4. Ten spies complained that giants were in the promised land and that they were too small to defeat them. What circumstances, excuses or giants stand in the way of your future?
5. Pray the prayer below asking God to help you keep your focus on His truth rather than the obstacles.

Prayer: Lord, I ask that your Holy Spirit would set off an internal alarm anytime I speak idle words or words of doubt that are contrary to your promise for me. I thank you that I have the mind of Christ and that you have victory in store for me! In Christ's name I pray. Amen.

- 10 -

Rewriting My Life Script

BY NOW, I'M SURE YOU GET IT. Your mouth is a megaphone. Your future is influenced by your affirmations. But if you're like me, you might need some help uprooting negative thoughts and creating new scripts.

If you've ignored your gut reactions…
Declare God's truth: I have the mind of Christ (1 Corinthians 2:16). I call on God and He answers me. He shows me great and mighty things I don't know (Jeremiah 33:3). I am led by His spirit (Romans 8:14) and He gives me an abundance of wisdom (James 1:5).

If you've thought you had to always prove yourself or be perfect…
Declare God's truth: I don't put confidence in my flesh (Philippians 3:4). Besides that, I'm already made perfect. (Hebrews 10:14). When I goof up, I know that God is for me and I don't have to defend myself (Proverbs 23:9). His grace is sufficient for me and His power is made perfect in my weakness (2 Corinthians 12:9-10).

If you've been convinced that what happened

was your fault...
Declare God's truth: I am in Christ, and now there is no condemnation (Romans 8:1). I've confessed my sins, and He's cleansed me from all unrighteousness (1 John 1:9). God has blotted out my transgressions and remembers them no more. Neither will I (Isaiah 43:25). I'm blameless in His sight and free from accusation. I stand before Him without a single fault (Colossians 1:22).

If you've thought boundaries were not necessary...
Declare God's truth: Above all else, God wants me to guard my heart (Proverbs 4:23). I don't vacillate or waver. I make up my mind and stick to it (2 Corinthians 1:17). I don't allow other people to cause division in my life (Titus 3:10).

If you've thought crazy is normal...
Declare God's truth: God wants me to live in peaceful dwelling places, in secure homes, in undisturbed places of rest (Isaiah 32:18). My mind is kept in perfect peace (Isaiah 26:3). God makes me dwell in safety (Psalm 4:8). My heart is not troubled (John 14:27). My ways please the Lord and He brings peace to my borders (Proverbs 16:7).

If you've been naïve or overlooked red flags

in relationships...
Declare God's truth: Actions really do speak louder than words (Proverbs 20:11). The simple believe anything, but I am prudent and give thought to my steps (Proverbs 14:15). I see danger and

take refuge. I refuse to ignore caution and pay the penalty (Proverbs 22:3).

If you've been too trusting...
Declare God's truth: God wants me to be cautious in friendships. I refuse to allow the way of the wicked to lead me astray (Proverbs 12:26). By their fruit I recognize those with evil intentions (Matthew 7:16a).

If you've helped others too much...
Declare God's truth: I help others when they are burdened, but I won't take over their responsibilities (Galatians 6:5). I don't help others to gain their approval (Galatians 1:10). I know the difference between one who is in need and one who is a sluggard (Proverbs 20:4). I don't allow slackers to wear me out (Proverbs 18:9).

If you've felt unworthy...
Declare God's truth: I am God's masterpiece (Ephesians 2:10). He loved me and gave Himself for me (Galatians 2:20). I am precious in His eyes (Isaiah 43:4). He created me on purpose for a purpose (Ephesians 2:10). I am enough (2 Corinthians 3:5).

MAKE YOUR MIND AND MOUTH AGREE

These scriptures are just a few to get you started. At the end of the chapter, I've written some more scripture scripts. You can use these to uproot some of the most common vain imaginations that the enemy uses to get you off track in relationships. Then, by using the acronym CAST, I'll show you how you can cast down idle accusations and speak life to your situation in four easy steps. When you make your mouth and mind agree with God's truth, you can eliminate castle cracks and reframe your future.

It's so important that we have God's word hidden in our heart. If we don't know what His word says about us, we won't recognize a lie when the enemy launches an attack. When his arrows pierce our mind, we won't know to remove it because our discernment is compromised. And when our judgment is anemic, we become vulnerable in the most significant way—we ignore the voice in our gut and the prompting of the Holy Spirit.

My friend, it's time to pay attention to your inner witness. When you learn to discern the voice of the Holy Spirit, you can begin to repair and eliminate the catastrophic castle cracks and the erosion they create.

IS YOUR HEART DECEIVING YOU?

Movies, media, love songs, romance novels, and dating sites all seem to give the same advice: When it comes to choosing a romantic partner, just follow your heart and, most of all, expect sparks to fly. But is that really good advice? Uncontrolled chemistry is dangerous. It can cause you to turn off wisdom. It can cause you to trust too fast and get hurt.

The subtle lie starts at an early age. Even cartoons and family-friendly movies send the message that romance happens instantly. Our culture associates the heart with our emotions. Even when it comes to making other important decisions, we often hear the same well-intended advice, "Just follow your heart."

It sounds good, but is following our heart a wise suggestion or a prescription for failure? Passages in the Bible don't seem to think it's such a good idea. For example, take Jeremiah 17:9. "The heart is deceitful above all things and beyond cure. Who can understand it?" And yet somehow we've still decided that our emotions provide strong wisdom. We've decided the heart is the place where we make wise choices.

This train of thought seems to be validated in modern Bible translations. For instance, in Psalm 16:7, the NIV translation: "I will praise the Lord, who counsels me; even at night my *heart* instructs me."

But wait a second. Listen to the same verse in the King James version: "I will bless the Lord, who hath given me counsel: my *reins* also instruct me in the night seasons."

Humans have reins? Hmmm. I thought reins were to steer horses.

Check it out. This is where it gets interesting. The word *reins* comes from the Hebrew word, *kil·yä'*. You may be surprised to find out what it means.

The kidneys.

Literally, reins refers to the physical organ of our kidneys. Webster's defines reins as any means of curbing, controlling, or directing; to check or restrain. Reins are used to control and direct.

So let's go back to the King James version of Psalm 16:7. "I will bless the Lord, who hath given me counsel: my *reins* also instruct me in the night seasons."

What the verse is really saying is this: I will bless the Lord, who has given me counsel: my *kidneys* also instruct me in the night seasons.

In other words, we should trust our gut—that feeling we get

when something doesn't seem right or seems too good to be true. When we can't put a finger on it, but we're hesitant. That's our gut instinct and the voice of the Holy Spirit trying to provide direction, discernment, or even a warning.

Our kidneys curb, control, and direct us. They give us the ability to check or restrain. They, not the heart, are the controlling and directing power in us. What if we could learn how to allow our kidneys, our gut and the seat of our emotions, to guide us before our heart deceives us? I think we can! We can learn how to trust our gut.

The function of our kidneys is interesting. They filter waste out of our body. They also filter blood before sending it back to the heart. This is how our kidneys are designed to protect our physical bodies. But what if they are also designed to protect us emotionally? What if God also designed our kidneys to filter out emotional waste before sending it on to our heart?

If we bypass our gut instincts and allow our reactions and thoughts to go unfiltered to our hearts, we jeopardize our ability to make wise decisions. Then our hearts take over and deceive us.

When we surrender our emotions and renew our mind, we have a wonderful promise. We will be able to test and approve what God's will is—his good, pleasing and perfect will (Romans 12:1-2).

Our heart doesn't do this. Our kidneys do.

We may not understand the gut instinct at first, but when we slow down, we'll be more apt to use caution so that we're not blindsided, caught off guard, or deceived. So pay attention. Don't be led by your emotions. Trust your gut.

"I knew something was wrong, but I couldn't put my finger on it," said Trisha. "All the tell-tale signs were there that Nathan was having an affair, but every time I thought about it, I tried to convince myself that I was wrong. I'd get these pings in my gut. Little things that he'd say that would make me think, hmm, that doesn't sound right. Too many things didn't add up. I tried so hard not to judge him. Sometimes he'd leave for days on end saying he needed some space. If I questioned him, he'd cuss me out and say I wasn't being a good Christian because I didn't trust him. I was a mess. I was so full of anxiety and false guilt, I couldn't see straight. But in the end, I'd agree with Nathan. I'd tell myself I was too judging and something must be wrong with me because I obviously had trust issues."

Trisha'd had an idyllic childhood with a father who adored her. Because of their wonderful relationship, she never imagined that a man could be anything but trustworthy. That was part of what made her vulnerable to Nathan's control and manipulation—she ignored her gut and was too trusting. She'd not yet learned that she had the right to trust her inner witness and choose her thoughts.

When Nathan's affairs were discovered and their relationship ended, Trisha told Nathan she would have no more contact with him. Still, she struggled with guilt. Thoughts bombarded her on a daily basis. Thoughts like, "Maybe I'm the one God wants to use to change him," or "Who will help save his soul if I don't?"

I like Trisha's word *ping*. It describes so well that little gut reaction when we feel like something isn't right. If we ignore the ping long enough, it doesn't go away. Instead it grows into a huge mess. A mess of humiliation, guilt, or shame. A mess of jealousy, disgust, or frustration. A mess of fear, insecurity, or doubt. Maybe you feel confused, overwhelmed, trapped, or crazy. These feelings are the result of destructive thoughts left unchecked that we give entrance into our castle.

Trisha is learning how to trust her gut and listen to the voice of the Holy Spirit. "Now I recognize that those pings in my gut are my intuition setting off an alarm, and I need to pay attention to them. The enemy still tries to use guilt tactics on me to try to convince me to take Nathan back. Now, I know I have a choice. If I fall for the guilt tactics, I know my peace will be destroyed and I'll invite the same mess right back in. When his lofty opinions try to wiggle their way back in my mind, I now use scriptures to replace his lies."

WHEN GOD'S WILL OVERRIDES YOUR WISHES

Like Trisha, sometimes we get pings in our gut that warn us about discord, disaster. or danger. But other times, the Holy Spirit guides us with God's direction and discernment for good things—His plan for our lives.

When God showed me that John was His pick for my husband, I'm thankful that I trusted His voice and not my own judgment. Before we were married, like most other women, I had my *list*. I knew what I wanted. *I* wanted someone older, sophisticated, and well established. Although John was nice, he didn't have any of those qualities. He was younger, warm and authentic, (I usually say goofy), and still in college—the exact opposite of what I was looking for.

Before you conclude I was a cougar dating a college guy, let me explain. John had been in the military for ten years and was discharged with a knee injury. After his discharge, he went back to school. We were both in our early thirties. Even though John is only two years younger than I am, I was looking for a man about five-years older. Left to my own romantic discernment, I would have overlooked John, but I'm thankful God knew my list was defective.

It was a Wednesday evening after work on January 28, 1998. I'd invited John over for dinner. I still had three young children, so going out to eat was more of a chore than a date. After dessert, we plopped down on the worn blue sofa in my TV room, where John asked, "Do you mind if I pray?" To this day, I don't remember what his prayer was about, but what happened next, I'll never forget.

An overwhelming presence of love and peace engulfed me, as if our souls were being knit together. I know it sounds cheesy, but it's the only way I can describe the supernatural experience that took place. I'd never felt that kind of love before, and I somehow knew that it was a foretaste of the kind of love I could have if I chose to trust God with the selection of my mate.

In the natural, I wouldn't have picked John. That divine witness, however, overruled all doubt. The next morning I marched in the office and announced to my single coworker, Julie, "I'm going to marry John." He hadn't even proposed, but I knew in my gut that John was God's pick, not mine. He wasn't just a good choice. He was God's choice.

My story can sound like a follow-your-heart kind of thing. For that reason, I want to make a disclaimer. Emotional highs in relationships can be so strong that we mistake them for divine direction. For one thing, the thought of marrying John was not my idea. I didn't swoon over John and ask God to bless my decision and then take an emotional connection as a confirmation that God validated my choice. If I had my way about it, I would have asked God to choose the other guy I was dating. That would have been a disaster!

The other point I'd like to make is the need to wait for confirmation on what you perceive as divine direction. I was convinced that God chose John for me, but I'd been wrong before. Because of my previous lack of discernment, I surrounded myself with wise counsel and waited for confirmations. I wanted peace to rule and refused to hurry. Over the next several months, God confirmed His will for our relationship in many convincing ways that I'll tell more about in later chapters.

PHYSICAL AND EMOTIONAL ALERTS

The next time you feel a ping in your gut, pay attention. The Spirit helps us in our weaknesses (Romans 8:26) and guides us into all truth (John 16:13). God's voice quickens our spirit, but you may also sense His guidance and instruction in other ways. You are a triune being. In other words, you're not just a spiritual being; you also have a soul and a body. Therefore, it's not uncommon that you may notice other types of pings—pings in your body and your emotions. These physical or emotional alerts come in a variety of forms.

If God is trying to warn you about something, some of the most common physical responses you may feel in your body include a knot in your stomach or a racing heart. Other physical responses may include a change in breathing patterns or tension in your body. Your forehead may scrunch or you might find yourself crossing your arms or changing your posture in an attempt to defend something you discern but can't yet see. These symptoms often seem insignificant. That's what can cause you to discount or ignore them.

You also need to pay attention to your emotions—the pings in your soul. How does your gut reaction make you feel? Ask the Holy

Spirit to give you discernment.

If the sensation in your body produces fear, take time to evaluate and listen. Is the fear a warning from God or an emotion produced by a vain imagination that you need to surrender? Don't just discount it because you assume that all fear is negative and needs to go.

When God is trying to give you direction about something positive, however, the emotional and physical responses may be different. Your eyes may widen in excitement and your body may feel a burst of energy. A sensation of joy may engulf you. Pay attention. You get into trouble when you let the voice of doubt derail divine direction. When God is trying to install vision, His plans are bigger than what we can accomplish outside of His strength. If thoughts like, "That would never work for me," or "It's too good to be true," assail you, it's a good indication that the enemy is trying to shut down what God wants to open up.

That's when it's important to slow down and examine your thoughts. You'll often make mistakes when you ignore your God-given intuition.

Talk-show host Oprah Winfrey said, "I've trusted the still, small voice of intuition my entire life. And the only time I've made mistakes is when I didn't listen."[14]

If the thought produces anger, sadness, confusion, despair, jealousy, hopelessness, or any other soul-destroying emotions, ask the Lord to help you surrender your thoughts to Him. Of course we all feel negative emotions from time to time, but we don't want to stay stuck there.

It's important to replace vain imaginations with a thought that will produce life. I call this the Philippians 4:8 test. If anything is true, noble, right, pure, lovely, or admirable, think on these things.

Emotional highs in relationships can be so **strong** that we *mistake* them for divine direction.

The more you prevent destructive thoughts from creeping into your castle, the more you will experience joy, safety, and freedom.

CAST DOWN VAIN IMAGINATIONS

Would you eat something poisonous? Unless you're a *Fear Factor* fanatic or a *Survivor* addict, I'm confident you'd say, "Of course not!" You know that poisonous food will make you sick. In a similar manner, poisonous thoughts poison our mind.

When toxic thoughts intrude our mind, we have a responsibility to cast them out. Sometimes it's difficult, however, to know which thoughts you should entertain and which you should give the boot.

"I feel so hopeless," said Trinity. "I don't know what's wrong with me. Every day, Trey is mad at me for something. I just can't seem to do anything right."

Trinity grew up in an abusive home where yelling and name-calling were common. "There probably wasn't a day that went by that my father didn't blame me for something and tell me I was dumber than a one-eyed monkey."

When she met Trey, she didn't think it was odd when he screamed at her or called her names. To her it wasn't just common behavior, it was the truth. Trinity believed a lie: if something went wrong, it must have been her fault.

Sometimes, like Trinity, we've been assaulted with lies for so long, they become embedded in our belief system. The lies aren't true, but because people that we trust or love tell us so frequently, we believe they must be true.

Here's where we can get stuck. If we don't recognize lies, we won't be able to replace them with truth. That's why it's important to pay attention to our negative emotions. If we're feeling hopeless like Trinity, or anxious, depressed, ashamed, or fearful, for example, often a lie is at the root.

We can't just erase bad thoughts, however. We have to discipline our minds to replace them. When I have thoughts that hinder my peace and confidence, I use **CAST**, a four-step process, to help me eliminate trash talk and transform it into truth. It stands for *Check, Appraise, Shift,* and *Treasure*.

The model is simple, but following it can't be a one-time thing. It must turn into a habit if you want to see permanent change. When a concerning thought comes to your mind:

CHECK *your gut*
Does the thought cause a reaction or tension in your body? Do you feel defensive? Nervous? A tightness in your stomach? Do you have racing thoughts? Often these and other physical symptoms serve as warnings that something isn't right. Pay attention to your body as well as your spirit.

APPRAISE *the emotion behind the thought*
Is the emotion unhealthy? If so…

SHIFT *your focus*
Find a scripture that speaks life and make your thoughts agree with God's word. Refuse to dwell on the vain imagination if it doesn't agree with what God says about you or your situation.

TREASURE *truth*
Keep it before you. Meditate on it. Visualize it. Ask God to show

you from His perspective what His truth looks like for you. Truth combined with meditation and vision is the most effective way to renew your mind.

Below is a list of common lies the enemy may whisper to you. Notice that the devil speaks in first person so you think the thoughts are your own. That's hogwash! He's just good at impersonating you.

- He said he was sorry, so I should trust him again.
- I should feel guilty for not helping him. It's my fault. I should try harder. I can change him.
- This is as good as it gets. Walk away from him, and I'll always be alone. I'm damaged goods. No man will ever want me. I'll never be good enough.
- My situation is hopeless.
- I'm trapped. There's no way out.
- I'll never get over my past.
- I always pick the wrong guy.
- The terrible things he says about me must be true.

When I first started learning how to renew my mind, I needed a cheat sheet. A list. A premeditated script so that when I was caught off guard and tempted to say what I saw, I had a plan. I wanted to know ahead of time how I'd respond so old habits wouldn't override my good intentions.

You've heard of premeditated murder. Every detail was planned in advance. That's what we're going to do. We're going to kill our giants! Here are some CAST examples and scripture scripts to show you how to renew your mind. It's time to destroy the evil whispers!

💣 When the voice of condemnation says, **"He said he was sorry so I should trust him again."**

> **Check** your gut: Do you feel a reaction or tension in your body? Your spirit?
>
> **Appraise** your emotions: Do you feel pressured, confused, worried, paralyzed, numb, weak? If so...
>
> **Shift** your focus: Meditate on these truths and say them out loud:
>
> I forgive, but trust must be earned. (1 John 3:18). I am not deceived by empty words (Ephesians 5:6) or a flattering tongue (Psalms 12:2). I am not naïve (Romans 16:18). Actions show what it is a man's heart (Proverbs 20:11). I don't fall for men who claim to know God, but deny Him by the way they live (Titus 1:16). I see danger and take refuge (Proverbs 27:12).
>
> **Treasure** the truth: How do these truths make you feel? Empowered, confident, in charge, full of courage, discerning? Now take a few moments and visualize yourself walking in truth.

💣 When the voice of condemnation says, **"I should feel guilty for not helping him. It's my fault. I should try harder. I can change him."**

> **Check** your gut: Do you feel a reaction or ten-

sion in your body? Your spirit?

Appraise your emotions: Do you feel bewildered, confused, worried, defensive, guilty, ashamed, inferior? If so…

Shift your focus: Meditate on these truths and say them out loud:

When others are foolish, it's not my job to pay the price (Matthew 25:8-9). Others ruin their life by their own foolishness (Proverbs 19:3). They are responsible for their own conduct (Galatians 6:5). Whoever scorns instruction will pay for it (Proverbs 13:13). We all have to give an account of ourselves to God (Romans 14:12). A hot-tempered man must pay the penalty; if I rescue him now, I'll have to do it again (Proverbs 19:19). When they won't listen, God gives men over to their stubborn hearts to follow their own ideas (Psalm 81:12).

Treasure the truth: How do these truths make you feel? Calm, secure, relaxed, relieved, trusting? Now take a few moments and visualize yourself walking in truth.

When the voice of condemnation says, **"This is as good as it gets. Walk away from him and I'll always be alone. I'm damaged goods. No man will ever want me. I'll never be good enough."**

Check your gut: Do you feel a reaction or tension in your body? Your spirit?

Appraise your emotions: Do you feel abandoned, vulnerable, inadequate, threatened, worried, rejected, helpless? If so…

Shift your focus: Meditate on these truths and say them out loud:

God's presence will always be with me (Psalm 139:7). He will not leave me or forsake me (Deuteronomy 31:6). I seek the Lord and I lack no good thing (Psalm 34:10). I am chosen. I am God's special possession (1 Peter 2:9). I am fearfully and wonderfully made (Psalm 139:14). I am God's masterpiece. He created me to do good things (Ephesians 2:10). He chose me before the creation of the world to be holy and blameless (Ephesians 1:4). As I delight myself in the Lord, He will grant me the desires of my heart (Psalm 37:4). I will not throw away my confidence; it will be richly rewarded (Hebrews 10:35). Whatever I ask in His name, the Father will give me (John 15:16).

Treasure the truth: How do these truths make you feel? Confident, secure, hopeful, safe, protected? Now take a few moments and visualize yourself walking in truth.

💣 When the voice of condemnation says, **"My situation is hopeless."**

Check your gut: Do you feel a reaction or tension in your body? Your spirit?

Appraise your emotions: Do you feel depressed, alone, tired, regretful, sad? If so…

Shift your focus: Meditate on these truths and say them out loud:

The Lord delivers me out of all of my troubles (Psalm 34:17). I am not afraid. Jesus has left me his peace (John 14:27). He will make me dwell in safety (Psalm 4:8). My hope is a strong anchor for my soul (Hebrews 6:19). The angel of the Lord encamps around me and because I fear Him, He delivers me (Psalm 34:7). God has plans to prosper me, not to harm me, plans to give me hope and a future (Jeremiah 29:11).

Treasure the truth: How do these truths make you feel? Safe, hopeful, encouraged, loved, important, valued, content? Now take a few moments and visualize yourself walking in truth.

💣 When the voice of condemnation says, **"I'm trapped. There's no way out."**

>Check your gut: Do you feel a reaction or tension in your body? Your spirit?
>
>**Appraise** your emotions: Do you feel helpless, scared, crazy, angry? If so…
>
>**Shift** your focus: Meditate on these truths and say them out loud:

The Lord will be my confidence and keep my foot from being snared (Proverbs 3:26). I give my burdens to the Lord, and He will take care of me. He will not permit me to slip and fall (Psalm 55:22). In my day of trouble, He will keep me safe (Psalm 27:5). If God is for me, who can be against me? (Romans 8:31). I dwell in the shelter of the Most High and will abide in the shadow of the Almighty. The Lord is my refuge and my fortress. He will deliver me from the accusations and traps of the enemy. Under His wings I will find refuge (Psalm 91:1-4).

Treasure the truth: How do these truths make you feel? Secure, safe, confident, encouraged, protected, accepted, calm, relaxed, trusting? Now take a few moments and visualize yourself walking in truth.

When the voice of condemnation says, **"I'll never get over my past."**

Check your gut: Do you feel a reaction or tension in your body? Your spirit?

Appraise your emotions: Do you feel devastated, hurt, controlled, frustrated, bitter, angry, resentful, cheated? If so…

Shift your focus: Meditate on these truths and say them out loud:

The Lord is close to me when I'm brokenhearted

and saves me when I'm crushed in spirit (Psalm 34:18). Even so I will not dwell on the past. God is doing a new thing in my life (Isaiah 43:18-19). I will not fear, for God is with me. I will not be dismayed, for He is my God; He will strengthen me and help me. He will uphold me with His righteous right hand (Isaiah 41:10). I can do all things through Christ's strength (Philippians 4:13). I am confident of this: I will see the goodness of the Lord in the land of the living (Psalm 27:13).

Treasure the truth: How do these truths make you feel? Loved, appreciated, valued, respected, encouraged, strong, hopeful? Now take a few moments and visualize yourself walking in truth.

When the voice of condemnation says, **"I always pick the wrong guy."**

Check your gut: Do you feel a reaction or tension in your body? Your spirit?

Appraise your emotions: Do you feel hopeless, humiliated, empty, alone, worthless? If so...

Shift your focus: Meditate on these truths and say them out loud:

I use wisdom and caution in relationships (Proverbs 12:26). God is my shepherd and I hear His voice (John 10:27). I am not deceived by a man's words. I pay attention to his actions and by his fruit, I recognize ungodly intentions (Matthew 7:16). I don't trust in myself. I walk in wisdom and I'm kept safe (Proverbs 28:26).

Treasure the truth: How do these truths make you feel? Wise, relieved, connected, grateful, enthusiastic, content, secure, hopeful? Now take a few moments and visualize yourself walking in truth.

💣 When the voice of condemnation says, **"The terrible things he says about me must be true."**

Check your gut: Do you feel a reaction or tension in your body? Your spirit?

Appraise your emotions: Do you feel stupid, humiliated, empty, depressed, ashamed, inferior, intimidated? If so…

Shift your focus: Meditate on these truths and say them out loud:

I should stay away from a fool, for I won't find knowledge on his lips (Proverbs 14:7). God will make peace my governor and righteousness my ruler (Isaiah 60:17). Instead of shame and disgrace, God has everlasting joy for me (Isaiah 61:7). I am no longer deserted, for the Lord takes delight in me (Isaiah 62:3-4). His grace is sufficient for me. When others insult me, his power is made perfect in me (2 Corinthians 12:9-10).

Treasure the truth: How do these truths make you feel? Complete, peaceful, joyful, excited, loved, appreciated, understood, respected, important, valued? Now take a few moments and visualize yourself walking in truth.

PONDER AND PRACTICE

I hope the above examples will help you make casting down vain imaginations a new habit. What other lies do you struggle with? Use the blanks below to write your own CAST script.

💣 When the voice of condemnation says, "_____
_____."

Check your gut: Do you feel a reaction or tension in your body? Your spirit?

Appraise your emotions: How do you feel?

Shift your focus: I will meditate on these truths and say them out loud:

Treasure the truth: How do these truths make you feel?

Now take a few moments and visualize yourself walking in truth.

💣 When the voice of condemnation says, "_____ _____."

Check your gut: Do you feel a reaction or tension in your body? Your spirit?

Appraise your emotions: How do you feel?

Shift your focus: I will meditate on these truths and say them out loud:

Treasure the truth: How do these truths make you feel?

Now take a few moments and visualize yourself walking in truth.

- 11 -

Setting Boundaries That Stick

"I CAN'T SEEM TO GET PAST THIS," Erica said. Collapsing in a heap, she covered her face. Long brunette locks with burgundy highlights fell past her shoulders. Gray roots exposed a lack of maintenance. Her two-carat solitaire sparkled in the stream of sunlight that flooded my office, making a contrast against her chipped manicure and thrift-store clothing.

"It's been two years since I found out that Steve was embezzling funds from his employer. I'm thankful his boss never filed suit, but I can't seem to let go."

Her voice softened. "The shame is overwhelming. We've lost everything and have had to start all over. Financially, our life is a mess, and I'm an emotional wreck. My jaw hurts every morning. I guess I'm clenching my teeth while I sleep, and I wake up exhausted." Erica bit her lip. "I want our marriage to work." She paused while a tear rolled down her cheek. She stared at the ceiling and whispered, "I gave him my heart. I put my trust in him. What now?"

I'd been working with Erica for a few months and sensed that she was ready to hear what I had to say. I took a piece of paper out of my printer tray and drew a picture of a teeter-totter. One seat was on the ground and the other seat was stuck up in the air. "I wonder if you've put your heart in the wrong place?" I said.

A look of shock washed over her face. "What do you mean?"

I drew two stick figures and put Erica's name near the figure stuck in the air. I put Steve's name near the figure seated on the ground. I put God's name near the fulcrum or the pivot point in the center.

"This is a picture of where you are now. The board of the teeter-totter represents your heart. The fulcrum that supports your relationship represents God. When you give all of your heart to Steve, your confidence and peace are controlled by what he does."

"That's exactly how I feel. For years I've been the one left hanging in midair. Steve has always controlled my peace. So how do I get it back? I want to be the one in charge!"

I drew another picture. This time Erica was in the seat on the ground and Steve was in the air.

"That looks more like it," Erica said.

"This is still not a good place to be," I said. "When you're in control, you're trusting in your own strength." I pointed to the fulcrum in the middle. "God's support means nothing when you put all your trust in yourself."

Erica let out a deep sigh. "So where am I supposed to put my heart?"

I pointed to the fulcrum in the middle of the teeter totter. "In the middle. Give it to God. A fulcrum is a pivot point. It's a support or point of rest. When you give all of your heart to God, you can rely on His support to allow you to love others. His supply of love never ends. When you give your heart to Him, He gives you the ability to love others so that even when they disappoint or betray you, you're not left stuck in the air. Your heart is kept protected and safe."

"That's where I want to be," said Erica. "How do I get there?"

GIVE YOUR HEART TO GOD AND YOUR LOVE TO OTHERS

It may sound romantic to give our heart to a man, but the Bible never tells us to give our heart to a person. It tells us to give our heart to God (Proverbs 23:26) and to trust in Him with all of our heart (Proverbs 3:5). Besides that, when we give all of our heart to someone else, we run the risk of making them an idol. We've also got to resist the urge to trust in ourselves or our own capacity and strength. When we do, the Bible calls us fools (Proverbs 28:26).

Like I explained to Erica, there's a place of balance—a place where we put our trust in God and allow Him to be the conduit of love to sustain our relationships. Proverbs 29:25 tells us that when we trust in the Lord, we're kept safe. So let's talk about how to find that place of trust and balance.

THE NEED FOR BOUNDARIES

Healthy boundaries create a moat around your property to protect your castle from unnecessary invasion. They may sound easy, but boundaries are one of the most misunderstood relationship topics. Most of the women I coach acknowledge the need for them, but many have no idea how to establish, articulate, and enforce them.

Maybe you've thought boundaries were selfish. That your priorities were to make him happy and ignore your own needs. Maybe you thought it was his job to protect your heart, not yours.

That if you loved him, there was no need to set boundaries. Then what did you do if you felt mistreated? Taken advantage of? Lied to? Often, the only way to squash the pain and injustice is to ignore it, minimize it, or deny it all together. But at some point, the volcano explodes. Anger stuffed inside has to come out somehow.

If you have a habit of ignoring your instincts or denying your emotions, your capacity to set healthy boundaries will be compromised. That's why the previous chapters spent so much time helping you identify invasive thoughts. This journey is progressive. Each step of building your castle helps make the next step easier.

Once you recognize that you've allowed men to take advantage of you, it might make you mad at yourself for tolerating unacceptable behavior. That's okay. Some anger is justified and can make you aware of the need for change. Just don't stay angry. Allow righteous anger to motivate you to make healthy changes, and then forgive yourself and move on.

Some women have grown up with the twisted notion that submission and surrender obligate them to say yes. That somehow it's godlier to be agreeable. Saying no, however, is a spiritual precept. Why? Because when we say yes when we really mean no, we have to clean up the mess of frustration and potential bitterness left behind. We are supposed to let our yes be yes and our no be no (Matthew 5:37). The good news is that we don't have to allow others to trespass against us. The Bible says, "Thou shalt love thy neighbor," not "Thou shalt please thy neighbor" (Mark 12:31).

If you've been mistreated, let me assure you: God is not happy. You didn't deserve it. And you don't have to continue to allow it. In her book, *The Emotionally Destructive Marriage*, Leslie Vernick says, "Jesus himself valued safety. He stayed away from certain places and

SETTING BOUNDARIES THAT STICK

people because he knew they meant to harm him (see John 7:11)."

When we don't protect ourselves physically or guard our hearts from emotional offenses, we often end up resentful and open the door to bitterness. Boundaries are not only biblical, they're necessary for our own freedom and the health of our relationships. If you struggle with any of the following boundary barriers, it's time to build a moat.

Look over the following list and consider how you typically respond. For example, do you *often, sometimes* or *never* feel guilty for saying no? In the margin, put an "o" for often, "s" for sometimes or "n" for never.

- ___ Feel guilty for saying no
- ___ Say yes when you really mean no
- ___ Say yes to gain his approval
- ___ Say no at first, but relent when he pesters you
- ___ Think his time is more valuable than yours
- ___ Say yes, but later change your mind
- ___ Say yes because you fear his reaction
- ___ Desire to be perfect
- ___ Feel responsible for him
- ___ Often feel overwhelmed with too many responsibilities
- ___ Overcommit because you think you can handle it
- ___ Think saying yes is more spiritual

Look over your answers, paying attention to how many times you put *often*. The more *oftens* you noted, the more you need to practice setting boundaries.

The Bible says, "Thou shalt *love* thy neighbor," not "Thou shalt *please* thy neighbor."

Setting Boundaries That Stick

Setting effective boundaries requires two things—communication and consequences. Your partner has to know what you expect, and he also needs to know how you intend to respond if he doesn't honor an expectation or violates your boundaries. You can't make him change, but his choice to comply with your wishes is often motivated by your behavior. When you continue to allow him to mistreat you, there's no reason for him to change.

Please hear me on this. A consequence is not a punishment or something you establish to discipline him. A consequence is something you create to protect your heart as well as the relationship. It communicates by your behavior, not by your complaints or persistent pleas, that you will no longer tolerate unacceptable behavior. It leaves him with the option to decide whether he wants to cooperate. Your motive to establish healthy boundaries is not to control him but to protect your heart from bitterness and resentment. Boundaries also help protect your relationship from the deterioration that will occur when mutual respect is not present.

In my marriage to my first husband, I was constantly frustrated because he left his socks and underwear on the floor. No matter how much I complained, he refused to put them in the hamper. It made me feel disrespected.

With the help of a mentor, I created a boundary statement—the way I would not only communicate my request but also state how I'd respond if it wasn't respected. Before I learned how to guard my heart, I thought I only had two choices: I could either be angry because I had to pick up Tom's things or I could be content because he complied. This mindset allowed him to control my peace of mind. Thankfully, my mentor helped me see other options.

I realized that I couldn't make Tom change, so if he didn't pick up his things, I still would because I wanted a neat home. So I told Tom that I'd be happy to do his laundry if he put his dirty clothes in the hamper. If I had to pick his things up, however, I'd put them in a different laundry basket and I would not do that laundry.

Guess what happened? Despite his persistent promises, Tom didn't change. Not one bit. He still didn't pick up his dirty clothes, but an amazing thing happened to *my* peace. I was no longer angry. I'd finally learned how to quit allowing his actions to control me.

This may seem like a trivial example, but, if we can't set boundaries for smaller irritations, we'll never be able to enforce more difficult boundaries. Over time, daily frustrations build into huge mountains of anger. Just like a small splinter causes much pain, it's the little foxes that spoil the vine. We have to stop the blood loss.

BE PREPARED

When setting effective boundaries, resist the temptation to verbalize idle threats. It's important to mentally prepare yourself to be ready to follow through with actions when others violate your boundaries. If you don't follow through, it only reinforces that you don't mean what you say. It takes time and determination to reroute how others treat you, but you can do it. Remember—say what you mean and mean what you say.

Authors Dr. Henry Cloud and Dr. John Townsend and The Boundaries Book Team posted this question in their blog post titled, *How to Test the Quality of any Relationship*: "Is it possible that others will become angry at our boundaries and attack or withdraw from us? Absolutely. God never gave us the power or the right to control how others respond to our 'no.' Some will welcome it; some will hate it.

"We can't manipulate people into swallowing our boundaries by sugarcoating them. Boundaries are a "litmus test" for the quality of our relationships. Those people in our lives who can respect our boundaries will love our wills, our opinions, our separateness. Those who can't respect our boundaries are telling us that they don't love our 'no.' They only love our 'yes,' our compliance."[15]

When your date, partner, or spouse ignores your boundaries, words alone will do nothing to convince him to change. Idle threats are meaningless. It takes time and determination to reroute how he treats you, so be patient and consistent. Don't give up.

There's a difference between being a peacemaker and being a peacekeeper. We are peacekeepers when we tolerate unacceptable behavior or when we try to keep the peace because we don't have the strength to stand up against abuse or disrespect. When we try to keep the peace, we're only creating temporary synthetic solace. We put Band-Aids on serious wounds and say there's peace when there really is none (Jeremiah 6:14).

But Jesus called us to be peacemakers. Being a peacemaker requires that we stand up to conflict so that we can make a permanent change. We have to take responsibility to change when other people violate our boundaries. Complaining or crying or giving long lectures and emotional pleas may elicit a promise or a temporary change, but they usually do nothing to create long-term changes.

Ignoring the situation and hoping it will go away or deciding to do nothing encourages continued disrespect. Covering up for his mistakes creates an illusion that everything is okay, but it's only a temporary salve that creates a deeper wound as time goes on. Proverbs 19:19 says, "A hot tempered person must pay the penalty;

rescue them, and you will have to do it again."

It may not seem fair, but we're the ones who have to make changes in the way we respond. We can't *make* them change, but we can teach them how to treat us by what we tolerate.

Bekah's two greatest needs in her marriage are to feel safe and chosen. Unfortunately, honoring those needs had not been a priority to her husband, Marcus. He golfs four times a week and is rarely home on weekends to spend time with their family. He drinks excessively and often stays out late, even when he promises to be home by a certain time. If she calls to find out where he is, he'll either ignore her or hurl insults to impress his drinking buddies within earshot.

Bekah gathered her courage and moved out. Within two weeks, Marcus had an affair. He blamed it all on her. "I wouldn't have done it, but you walked out on me."

Marcus's accusations that his affair was all her fault filled her with a false sense of guilt. Devastated, Bekah moved back in when he promised to change. Instead of change, however, he got worse.

If we set a boundary before we're emotionally ready, it'll be difficult to resist the backlash. That's why it's important to be resolved. Don't communicate a boundary until you're prepared to follow through with the consequences.

Communicating effective boundaries and deciding what consequences we're willing to enforce requires a lot of thought and prayer. It's a difficult process. Especially when we were hoping that he'd be the one to change. It may not seem fair to know that we're the ones who have to take active measures to change the dynamics of our marriage or relationship, but it's necessary.

Bekah and I met to go over how she would articulate a reasonable boundary. We started out by discussing an upcoming business trip that she would be attending with her husband. We worked on creating a boundary statement—the way she would articulate her desires and how she'd respond if they weren't respected.

It's important to do this ahead of time. As you learn to express your own boundary statements, take the time to consider if you're being reasonable as well as if you're resolved to follow through. It helps to brainstorm options with a wise friend. When emotions are elevated, it's hard to think with clear focus. After you've decided how you'll communicate your wishes as well as how you'll respond if he doesn't respect them, practice saying them out loud until you can say state your desires with a calm demeanor. You don't want to cower under the pressure of the moment or back down because of threats or verbal abuse.

I suggested that Bekah begin her conversation with Marcus with a positive affirmation. An accusation like, "You never do this!" would only create a negative environment and put Marcus in a defensive posture.

Here's what Bekah came up with:

"I'm glad that you're invested in working on our marriage, and I'm really looking forward to our upcoming trip together. I believe it will be a great new start for us. As you know, in the past it's hurt me tremendously when you said you were coming home at a certain time but stayed out late drinking. It made me feel disrespected and not valued.

"I do believe that you're committed to making changes in this area, but the only way for me to know for sure is to see that evidenced by your behavior.

"Just to let you know in case that happens on our trip, I'm

choosing to change the way I normally respond, and, if you don't honor your commitment, I won't be in the room when you get back. Those kinds of actions communicate that you're not invested in making me feel safe and chosen. I realize I can't make you come home on time, but I can change my own responses.

"I also won't tolerate sarcastic or accusatory reactions. If those happen, I won't participate in the other planned events or may choose to fly home early."

This was a game changer for their relationship. Working through the need to communicate her needs to her husband instead of allowing her anger to pile up freed Bekah. "My value and confidence soared—not because he gave it to me, but because I gave it to myself. Until I stood up for me, I never realized how much I'd backed down because of fear."

Bekah's story ended well. The more confident she became, the more Marcus honored her wishes. That's not always the case. Not all men have the character or motivation to change. But even if they don't, you'll grow stronger and less tolerant of unacceptable behavior. One thing is certain. If you don't grow, neither will your relationship. If you continue to accept unacceptable behavior, he'll continue to treat you the same.

WORDS OF WISDOM

Below are some of my favorite scriptures that show God's heart on healthy boundaries. As you read through the verses, ask yourself which ones most speak to you. Consider why. Also consider how you can use this wisdom and instruction in your own relationships.

- ✧ Above all else, guard your heart, for everything you do flows from it (Proverbs 4:23).
- ✧ A hot-tempered person must pay the penalty; rescue them, and you will have to do it again (Proverbs 19:19).
- ✧ Do not speak to fools; for they will scorn your prudent words (Proverbs 23:9).
- ✧ Whoever corrects a mocker invites insults; whoever rebukes the wicked incurs abuse (Proverbs 9:7).
- ✧ Drive out the mocker, and out goes strife; quarrels and insults are ended (Proverbs 22:10).
- ✧ Stay away from a fool, for you will not find knowledge on their lips (Proverbs 14:7).
- ✧ The one who gets wisdom loves life (Proverbs 19:8a).
- ✧ The fear of the Lord leads to life; then one rests content, untouched by trouble (Proverbs 19:23).
- ✧ Like a muddied spring or a polluted well are the righteous who give way to the wicked (Proverbs 25:26).
- ✧ Fear of man will prove to be a snare, but whoever trusts in the Lord is kept safe (Proverbs 29:25).
- ✧ Warn a divisive person once, and then warn them a second time. After that, have nothing to do with them (Titus 3:10).
- ✧ Have no fear of sudden disaster or of the ruin that overtakes the wicked, for the Lord will be at your side and will keep your foot from being snared (Proverbs 3:25-26).
- ✧ In the paths of the wicked are snares and pitfalls, but those who would preserve their life stay far from them (Proverbs 22:5).

PONDER AND PRACTICE

1. Who in your life do you have the most difficulty setting boundaries with?
2. List three situations in the past where you've felt manipulated by this person.
3. How did you feel? How did you respond?
4. If this situation were to reoccur, write out how you could respond in a healthier way. Include the following:
   - Your boundary statement
   - The consequence or repercussion you'll enforce if he disrespects your boundary
   - How you anticipate his initial reaction to your boundary statement and repercussion
   - How you'll calmly respond to his pushback without defending yourself

- 12 -

SPOT AND STOP MANIPULATION

A MAN'S FAITH AND COMMITMENT to Christ are among the most important character qualities to the women I coach. If faith is not important to a man, it's a deal breaker. And it should be. But since so many wolves in sheep's clothing use faith as bait, how do you know if a man's motives are genuine? Is he the real deal or a counterfeit Christian?

I hear it over and over in my coaching practice. "But he *said* he was a Christian!"

Well…words are cheap. The mouth has to match the motives, and the only way to discern whether or not a man's motive is genuine is to watch and wait. It's vital that you forgo emotional involvement until you *know*: Is his motive genuine, or is he mirroring you to mislead you?

A man who mirrors you looks at you and studies you. Then he does his best to act like your reflection in order to gain your trust. Mirroring is a manipulative strategy to bait women who are unaware, naïve, trust too soon, don't inquire of the Lord, or are in a hurry for a relationship. You can't rush trust.

The story in the fourth chapter of Ezra is a great example of men who claim to be godly in order to gain control—men who study their prey, find out what is most important to them, and copy their behavior in order to camouflage their own intent. Men who use this technique only claim to be Christians in order to gain control.

When the enemies of Judah and Benjamin heard that the exiles were building a temple for the Lord, they offered to help. "Let us help you build because, like you, we seek your God and have been sacrificing to him" (Ezra 4:2).

Boloney!

They tried to convince the exiles that they worshipped the same God, but it was only lip service.

When the people of Judah answered that they wanted to build it by themselves, their enemies did an about face. They set out to discourage them and make them afraid to go on building. They even hired counselors to work against them and frustrate their plans.

Can you say devious? Can you say control and manipulation?

The story is a great example of the mirror motive. In a new relationship, not all men who claim to serve the Lord really do. In fact, as this story showcases, when they don't get what they want, they turn around and work against you. Men with false motives often use Christianity as a cover to get what they want. They use the faith connection to establish a facade of trust and intimacy so that they can later build a platform of control.

They'll text you a good morning message and throw in the praying hands emoji or say something like, "May God bless your day!" They'll sprinkle the conversation with a devotional they read. They may have read the devotional, but their motive was only to impress you with their spiritual commitment.

They aren't legit. They're counterfeit.

That's why in relationships it's so important not to fall for what men say. Men who are manipulative are great at mirroring. They'll find out what your highest priorities and passionate interests are, and in an effort to woo you, they'll claim to have the same ambitions. It's a way of establishing common ground. One of the greatest tactics is using faith to create a strong bond.

They think it's easy to mislead Christians. Not because we lack wisdom, but because one of the foundations of our faith is trust. But blind trust gets us into trouble. Salt looks just like sugar, so do your due diligence.

When we ignore the promptings of the Holy Spirit and give our trust away to a man who is not trustworthy, it takes time to get over the pain. But that doesn't mean all men are like that. It's up to us to use caution and discernment and ultimately to put our trust in God. All relationships will disappoint us at some point, because none of us is perfect. When men have hurt us in the past, however, was it because we overlooked character flaws and gave our trust away before it was earned? If that was the case, take it slow next time and pay attention to yellow flags. They always come before the red flags. When we give trust away without testing the character of a man, it's like running out on a frozen pond. Will the ice support us, or will it crack?

Maybe you think it's awkward to examine a man's character. It's somehow not the Christian thing to do. You may feel like you're being judgmental. Let me just say this—it's a must. You're not judging his eternal destiny. You're evaluating his behavior to ensure that he's trustworthy, honorable, and relationship-ready.

It's imperative that you do this before you get emotionally involved. Otherwise, the thrill of a new relationship will distort your discernment. In his book, *Finish: Give Yourself the Gift of Done*, Jon Acuff says, "Your emotions cloud your judgment. They form a perfect smoke screen for denial, making your path in life feel murky and confusing. In the fog of feelings, it's hard to see what's really happening."[16]

Take it slow and be realistic. Making decisions based on your emotions is dangerous. By the time you notice areas of incompatibility, the discomfort of leaving is often too strong to end the relationship. Your desire to stay may override the wisdom to leave, because discontentment becomes familiar. Like quicksand, it's a slow drown.

You'll also want to consider his maturity. Keep in mind that age does not make a man mature. Character does. Gauging character suitability takes time and intentional consideration, so don't be gullible and believe everything he says.

Wise woman are cautious in friendship (Proverbs 12:26). You're trying to decide whether or not a man is a suitable investment for the most valuable asset you own—your heart. Is he capable of a healthy relationship now? Not in the future—with a bit of persuasion and work. But now. Be careful not to fall for potential. Potential is like peanut butter. It's nutty and sticks to the roof of your mouth.

IS HE A FIT?

If you want more wisdom on how to evaluate character, get my Relationship Risk Assessment, which has tons of tips on how to spot yellow flags in relationships. You can also take the quiz to find out how well a man stacks up in regards to thirty-three different character qualities. Get it all by downloading *Foolproof Ways to Know if*

Spot and Stop Manipulation

He's Right for You at www.isheafit.com.

One way to test a man's motives is to see how he handles disagreement. A controlling man won't stand for it. But if you always agree with him, you'll never be able to detect deceit.

Alexa's first several dates with Austin were full of engaging conversation. He was quick-witted and intelligent. In between dates, he pursued her with consistent texts and made sure he called her once a day. He made it clear that he was interested in dating only her and made a great effort to take her out on interesting dates to her favorite coffee shops, bookstores, and hiking spots. But she wasn't sure if his determination was genuine confidence or rooted in a calculated attempt to win her over so he could control her. She'd been down that road before.

Alexa decided to test Austin's reaction to her contrary opinion. Would he respect her opinion or contest it? She also decided to change plans at the last minute to see if he'd react in anger or show patience and flexibility.

Alexa was using wisdom. In any new relationship, you must use sound judgment. It's important to find ways to test whether or not a man has respect for you and your opinions. Find opportunities to politely disagree with him or tell him no. Pay attention to how he responds. You're not doing this to be antagonistic but to evaluate whether or not he will respect your wishes or try to control you. Someone who only likes you if you have the same opinion or are always agreeable will likely not honor your boundaries.

SPIRITUAL FAITH FUZZIES

Men who are skilled at mirroring use spiritual faith fuzzies to warm your heart. They know that faith is a powerful intimacy connector. Not only does it connect you on a soul level, but sharing a faith connection builds a platform for a spiritual connection. That's why if they know your faith is important to you, men who are controlling and manipulative will use scripture and faith as a way to establish instant intimacy and worm their way into your heart.

These men seek out women who have weak boundaries. Like a puppet and a puppeteer, the relationship works well until the puppet decides to cut the strings. When the cords are cut, the puppeteer feels threatened and angry. They'll do everything in their power to restring the puppet.

After two failed abusive marriages, April continued to gravitate toward charming men. By the time she realized how deceitful Brandon was, she was in deep. He drank heavily, and she caught him lying about being with other women. But he was going to church with her and said all the right things about wanting to change.

She believed his words over his actions. She called the relationship off several times, but Brandon pursued her with the tenacity of a lion after its next meal. Reluctantly, April gave him several more chances.

"He wouldn't leave me alone. He knew where I hung out, and he'd show up and beg to talk. He'd come to church and sit right next to me. I couldn't tell him to move…at church."

April tossed her long brunette locks over her shoulder. "Then I'd wonder—what if he really had changed? He keeps telling me that he's going to counseling. Maybe I should reconsider. What if I'm wrong?"

Even though April continued to see social media posts of Brandon partying with other women, he charmed her into believing he was changing. Plagued by self-doubt, April went back and forth with him for over two years.

When a surge of reality would hit, April would have a final talk with Brandon and block his number on her phone. But the breakup never stuck. Brandon would hunt her down, pressure her to talk after church and convince her of his sincerity. Then she'd feel guilty and unblock him again.

Calling off the relationship for good was beyond April's comfort zone. She worried about being judgmental and felt guilty for not believing the best in him. She worried about not honoring God's call to love. To be patient, to bear one another's burdens, to keep no record of wrongs. She didn't know how to honor God's word without being a doormat. Why?

Because as a physician's assistant, April's core strengths were kindness, compassion, and mercy. The perfect recipe for Satan to twist into his own version of a Christian concierge—one who serves the rude, self-seeking, arrogant demands of another.

Satan is a master at perverting our greatest strengths and using them against us. He longs to turn us into puppets, pulling our strings so we'll never find the freedom we're meant to have. He strangled April's kindness and convinced her that to be firm and assertive was to be aggressive and rude. Standing up to Brandon and ending the relationship made her feel judgmental.

Satan twisted her compassion and magnified it into a sense of false guilt. Then he transformed her mercy into a mountain of self-doubt that prevented her from closing the door on the relationship. As a result, Brandon didn't take her seriously.

Until April had enough.

"Brandon didn't believe me until I believed myself first," said

April. "I got tired of him pulling me back and forth and decided to block him for good. It was scary, but it felt liberating to let go. It was through this struggle that I grew into me. I'm no longer a puppet. I cut the strings."

Men who are used to being in control won't easily surrender. They'll put up the biggest fight in the beginning to see if you're serious. Right after a breakup or building a boundary is the hardest time to maintain your resolve, but if you stick through it, it will get easier. You have to mean what you say. The only way he'll believe you is if your actions confirm your words. When he protests, don't argue with him or try to reason with him.

If he mocks you or uses sarcasm, don't correct him. You'll only invite more insults (Proverbs 9:7). It's not worth your time to try to reason with insanity. Just follow through with what you said you'd do. You'll never change what you're willing to tolerate.

JUST SAY NO

One of the most powerful and yet the most overlooked boundaries is the short two-letter word—*no*. If you tend to say yes without thinking, it's important to practice taking a pause before you respond to a request. Before you say yes, take a moment and do a heart check. How do you feel? Does the request make you feel happy or does it feel like an imposition? Do you have a pit in your stomach? Do you feel appreciated or taken advantage of? Respected or disrespected?

If you sense any hesitation, don't say yes, at least not yet. Only say yes if you can do it with a happy heart. If you get that nagging feeling in your gut, it's best to say no.

Take some time to consider your decision. There's nothing

Spot and Stop Manipulation

wrong with saying, "Let me think about it." Or, "Let me get back with you on that."

Saying yes when you really don't want to will cause you to get frustrated with yourself for the over-commitment, but it'll also create tension and resentment between you and your partner.

Maybe you've made a habit of saying yes in order to maintain the peace. If you deny his request and it makes him mad at you, this should be a red flag—he's using anger to control you. Don't say yes in order to gain approval or to please him. That's the wrong reason to say yes. Contrary to what you may believe, saying no is not a rude reply.

The New York Times bestselling author, Jon Acuff, says, "If you tell someone 'no' and they react in anger, they just confirmed you made the right decision."[17]

When men are accustomed to our compliance, they'll continue to take advantage of our graciousness and accommodation until we put a stop to it. If you never say no, you'll never grow. When you accept the responsibility to take care of yourself, it will set you free. When you recognize the part you play in allowing a man to dominate or control you, you can be liberated by another revelation: If you allowed it, you can also put a stop to it—just by saying, "No!"

Your relationship will benefit from putting boundaries in place. Boundaries allow you to take care of yourself and prevent anyone from taking advantage of you. The most spiritual thing you'll ever learn how to do is to say "no" and not feel guilty.

If you respect yourself first, you'll have less conflict in relationships because resentment will not stand in the way. Saying yes may feel like the godlier choice, but when it causes you to walk in frustration or unforgiveness, saying yes when you mean no is a sin

You'll never *change* what you're willing to *tolerate.*

you commit against yourself.

DON'T DEFEND

"I was never allowed to have boundaries as a kid," said Jen, "so as an adult, I didn't recognize someone was violating them.

"Once when I was about five, my parents had a friend over to the house. They wanted me to sit in his lap, but I didn't want to. For some reason, he seemed creepy. I got a huge scolding and was taught that my behavior was rude. That day I learned that I had no authority over my body. It was wrong to protest an invasion of my personal space. Good girls didn't say no. That belief grew up with me.

"When I started dating, I didn't know how to oppose unwanted sexual advances. I'd never learned how to say no. Instead, I just sucked it up.

"Even after I was an adult my mother interrogated me, and I felt obligated to defend my decisions. I didn't know that there was another way. I thought in order to justify my choices, it was necessary to give full disclosure for everything I did."

This brings up another point about saying no. You don't have to defend, justify, or explain yourself. Even Jesus spoke this truth when he said, "All you need to say is simply 'Yes' or 'No'; anything beyond this comes from the evil one" (Matthew 5:37).

When you're used to giving explanations for your choices, however, just saying *no* can seem foreign. Your brain is trained to explain.

That's why it's helpful to craft gentle but wise responses ahead of time so you won't cave under the pressure of the moment or react out of anger. Remember, you're doing this to preserve your peace so that you don't wind up aggravated and bitter because you're doing something you wish you had said no to. Resist the urge to explain or defend yourself. The more you explain, the more ammunition you'll give him to protest. A simple no will do. No apology. And don't make up an excuse. That will just beg other questions that will bait you right back into defending and explaining.

One of the easiest ways to prevent protests is to redirect the conversation right after you say no. If you don't, you've just given him the ball, so to speak, and he'll throw the conversation right back to you with more baiting questions. So take charge of the dialogue. Take a look at the following example to see what I mean.

Let's say that your spouse calls you at work at 4:45 and says, "I know I said I'd pick up the kids from daycare, but the guys want to meet for a game of basketball. Can you pick them up again tonight?"

You don't want to. You'd planned to come home and relax for a bit. It's his turn, and he has a habit of calling at the last minute.

If your answer is, "No, I can't," it will beg him to ask, "Why not?" Then you'll put yourself in a position where you have to defend your decision. Instead, be direct. A better response would be, "Oh, that's too bad, but I plan to go straight home." Then immediately redirect the conversation with something like, "What sounds good for dinner?"

If he interrupts you and says, "Please, just this once?" Remember to stay on track. Just ignore his question and continue along with the question you asked. "I was thinking about chicken and mashed potatoes. Does that sound good?"

Do you see where I'm going with this? You are taking charge of the conversation by steering it in a different direction. In the process, you're refusing to take his bait to get you to explain yourself, get into a disagreement, or reconsider his request because he's worn you down again.

Don't complain. Pointing out the fact that he frequently tries to avoid his responsibilities at the last minute will only make you sound like a whiner and open the door for a conflict. Overlook the opportunity to engage. If you don't, your conversation will merge into a debate and he'll never take your *no* seriously. There is a time for that discussion, but this isn't it. Right now, you're staying focused.

Don't apologize. Don't say, "No, honey, I'm sorry, I can't." You're not sorry, so there's no need for an apology. You already had an agreement, so you don't owe him an excuse. If it will make you angry that he manipulated the situation again, a yes will lead to bitterness and relationship discord. It's your job to say no.

If this seems too hard to do with your partner, practice this tactic with friends or co-workers who try to take advantage of you. It's easier to say no to people with whom you don't have a strong emotional connection. When you practice saying no to casual acquaintances or co-workers, it will become easier to stand up for yourself in romantic or intimate relationships.

When we're strangled by the fear of telling others no, we pile frustration on ourselves and our relationships. We pay a price when we base our own worth on pleasing others. Fear of man proves to be a snare, but in the end, we gain more favor when we don't back down (Proverbs 28:23).

No one says your partner has to agree with all of your decisions. If you find your worth by always trying to make him happy, you'll end up as a doormat. You can be assertive without being aggressive. You'll obtain more respect from him and create more personal peace with yourself when you learn how to say no and stick to it.

PONDER AND PRACTICE

1. Think of a situation in which you wanted to say no or stand up for yourself but didn't. Maybe you were put on the spot, caught off guard, or pressured into doing something you didn't want to do. What were the circumstances?
2. How would you imagine a strong and confident woman would handle a similar situation?
3. How could you handle a similar situation next time?
4. Now, take some time to imagine how you want the dialogue to go next time someone makes a request you want to say no to. Write out your responses to the protests you imagine. Preparation and practice are the best ways to develop healthy habits and will prevent you from being caught off guard again.

- 13 -

Where is the Holy Spirit in All of This Chaos?

AFTER MY AFFAIRS WERE discovered in my first marriage, the madness got worse. Tom's addiction grew to insane levels. He knocked off a bottle of fifty pain pills the next weekend. In desperation, I called Pastor Dan, who talked him into going to rehab; but after two days, Tom demanded to be released. Without anything to anesthetize my anger and despair, I was desperate for help. How could our marriage survive? How was I going to get Tom off drugs? I only knew one other person who might be able to help.

I had met Barbara in an Al-Anon meeting, a group I used to attend when Tom went to AA meetings. When I first met Tom, he'd said he'd been clean from drugs for a couple of years. He went to AA meetings almost every day. Often I tagged along with him, but after several months of enduring the circle of introductions where everyone said, "Hi, my name is So-and-So, and I'm an alcoholic," I finally realized I belonged in the *other* group—a woman's group with mysterious ladies who talked about things I'd never heard of.

The Al-Anon ladies were a weird bunch. Their meetings focused on topics like detaching, letting go, boundaries, and the f-word—forgiveness.

When it was your turn to talk, there were rules. You couldn't focus on the problem or the horrible things your alcoholic or addict did. "We've all tried changing others," they'd say. "But we've learned the futility of that. We can only change ourselves. Let our discussion be focused on solutions for our own behavior instead of trying to fix someone else."

I wasn't interested in changing. I'd held firm to the belief that if Tom would just get his act together, I'd be fine. He was the problem. I sat in those meetings for two years, clueless about how to embrace the peace they talked about.

Until I was drowning in despair and could no longer find anything to cover my pain.

The Sunday after Tom found out about my fall from grace, we sat on the pew seething at each other. Going up for prayer was out of the question. The prayer line was for normal requests. Clean prayers. Prayers for stuffy noses and children. Not for addiction, pornography, or adultery. I wouldn't dare go forward.

From my perspective, the people we went to church with had perfect marriages. They were the real Christians, and we were the outcasts. I didn't think anyone would possibly understand what I was going through. Except maybe Barbara. I saw her sitting a few rows in front of me. Out of the two thousand people in the auditorium, she might have been the only one who would understand.

After service, I chased her out to the parking lot.

"BARRR-BRA!" I yelled. I could almost hear an echo from my frantic scream.

She glanced my way, and I ran to her car. Out of breath with tears welling up in my eyes, I begged, "Will you take me to an Al-Anon meeting?"

Where is the Holy Spirit in All of This Chaos?

The next Saturday, Barbara and I slid into metal folding chairs with the other ladies in the circle. It was a cold February morning. At nine-thirty sharp, the chairman began the meeting. "Today's topic is courage."

In unison the circle of ladies all opened their ODAT books (a topical devotional book based on the acronym One Day at a Time) to the index of subjects.

"Who'd like to read and share?"

A lady with dark brown hair raised her hand and began to read. "'I will not fall in with the alcoholic's [in my case, the addict's] craving for punishment to relieve his guilt. I will not scold and weep, for it will not help me overcome the difficulties we are trapped in. I will try very hard to deal with my day by day difficulties with quiet poise, remembering always that I am doing this for my own benefit.'"[18]

The lady with the brown hair kept talking while the phrase, *I'm doing this for my own benefit*, bounced back and forth within my mind.

I glanced outside the window. A robin poked the ground looking for worms, unconcerned that the ice-covered patches had not yet melted. The robin seemed content despite the frigid temperatures that made her job three times as hard. She wasn't waiting until spring for relief.

Watching her pound the ground with determined resolve, I wondered, *could I be content despite my husband's addiction?*

The brown-haired lady continued, "I used to think that the only way I could be happy was if Danny was sober. But I've learned to take responsibility for my own happiness. Now I know…the only person who can make me happy is me."

A ray of sunshine sparkled through the window as truth flooded my mind. For the first time in two years of attending meetings with the weird ladies, I understood what they were talking about.

I couldn't fix Tom. Oh, how I'd tried. I'd exhausted all of my own efforts to find peace and failed. But at that point, my desperation produced a willingness to change.

For the rest of the meeting, I absorbed every word those ladies said. And the weirdness melted.

I was now one of them.

And on that cold February morning, despite the fact that my world was crumbling around me, I wanted to learn how *I* could change. No longer would I give Tom permission to rule my happiness, my peace, and my joy.

That day sunshine shocked my soul, and I embraced the courage to change. Not to change Tom, but to change myself. The journey of a thousand miles begins with one step and I…

I was on my way.

A CRYSTAL CLEAR CHANDELIER

When revelation invades a soul, it produces light. All of a sudden, a switch flips and a thousand beams bounce off crystal facets and flood our castle with a luxurious radiance. We see things we've never noticed before. Fear melts as the darkness scatters. Courage rises up as shadows evaporate. We're now in charge, and we wonder why we've lived so long in opacity.

Once the lights come on, we never want to live in darkness again. Even with the brightest chandeliers, however, we still have to change burnt-out light bulbs from time to time. Nothing burns out light bulbs faster than denial and unmet expectations.

Let's talk about denial first. Sometimes you may not be aware of denial. So, I'd like you to take a moment and be honest with yourself. How do you feel right now? When you think of the men who have hurt you, does a feeling of angst still wash over you? Is there a nagging disappointment that you've tried to bury? It's awful to keep dragging the pain around with you. It gets heavier each year. But here's the truth.

Denial will get you nowhere.

Without an honest appraisal of your life, *nothing* changes. When memories or marriages get messy, you may think it's easier to pack up the pain and move on. But if you carry the bricks of your past into your next relationship, you'll keep building the same castle. When you exhaust all of your own resources to cover the pain, you'll find that your desperation has produced a treasure—a willingness to see things in a different light.

When the light of the Holy Spirit illuminates your soul, it shows on the outside. You no longer feel vulnerable and helpless, and as a result, you no longer look vulnerable and helpless. It translates a message to others. You're strong and confident, no longer depressed, hopeless, humiliated, or ashamed. Feelings of inadequacy and rejection are gone. You're no longer abandoned and paralyzed. You're content, empowered, and alive. When you value who you are, you're no longer controlled by others' opinions of you. You begin to respect yourself, and the good news is that respect is contagious. Others will begin to respond to you differently because you no longer tolerate disrespect.

Trust me. The work of releasing denial and facing reality is worth it. When denial no longer dims the light in your castle, there's an added bonus. It's easier to change the unrealistic expectations that have hindered your freedom.

CHANGING UNREALISTIC EXPECTATIONS

Unrealistic expectations are a down payment on resentment. They grow when we trust too much or too soon. It's like driving a car even though we know the brakes are worn out. We hope anyway. It's like leaving the house without an umbrella when storm clouds loom. We assume the risk and take our chances.

In my marriage to Tom, I was naïve and unprepared. I didn't recognize the risk. I didn't realize that I'd handed over the key to my happiness, contentedness, and peace to my husband. He was like a car with no brakes. But once I climbed in and buckled the seatbelt, I gave him control over my every emotion. His actions dictated whether or not I felt safe and secure or weak and worried. It was as if we were Siamese twins, and I was stuck.

If he was high, I felt ashamed and hopeless.

If he was hostile and belligerent, I felt trapped and afraid.

If he was out of work, I was out of my mind with worry.

Even when things seemed good, there was unrest. If he was sober and employed, I felt temporary stability, but lurking in the background was a nagging fear—*how long would it last?*

When our expectations are aimed at someone who is incapable of meeting them, it's like going to a muffler shop for a muffin. We put ourselves in the path of defeat and end up disappointed every time. I want you to understand, however, that changing your expectations doesn't mean that you need to lower your expectations. I know that sounds like the same thing, but it's not. I think I can best

If you carry the **bricks** of your past into your next relationship, you'll **keep** building the same castle.

explain what I mean by allowing you to hear a conversation I had with Barbara.

One day I called Barbara sobbing about an argument I had with Tom. Tom was in sales and controlled his own hours, but his work ethic played third fiddle to his love for sleep and leisure. It was the same song and dance for years. Our bills racked up. I freaked out. He made empty promises to change and work harder.

The day before, my anger exploded. It was two o'clock in the afternoon, and he hadn't budged from the couch—a common practice for him. After my emotional confrontation, he made the same pledge that he made each time my temper flared. "You're right, honey. Tomorrow will be different. I've got several appointments lined up, and I'll be out of the house by eight-thirty."

For some stupid reason, with great expectations, I believed him again. But the next day, after I got the kids off to school and started laundry, I glanced at the clock. It was ten o'clock, and Tom was still in bed. Filled with rage, I burst into the bedroom in tears. I ripped off the covers and demanded that he get up. Of course, that didn't play out well. A stream of curse words and vial comments about my ungrateful attitude sprayed out of his mouth like bullets from a machine gun.

Furious, I grabbed the car keys and headed to the pay phone down the street. This was back in the day where landlines ruled the world, and our phone had been cut off since we were behind on our payment.

After I explained the scenario to Barbara, she paused for a moment before she began. "Christy, I've seen a pattern in how you react to Tom. I understand his actions are inappropriate and that you're scared about what's going to happen. But you can't change

Tom and neither can I. So let's talk about how you can change your expectations."

My eyes widened. "Change my expectations? I don't want to do that! I *expect* him to go to work! I *expect* him to take care of his family and pay the bills!"

"But your expectations, while reasonable, are not realistic given Tom's character. I'm not telling you to *lower* your expectations. I'm telling you to *change* them. There's a difference."

I threw my hand in the air and gasped. "I don't understand! What do you mean?"

"If you keep expecting Tom to honor his empty promises, you're going to continue to be frustrated and angry. Do you want to live in a continual state of anger?"

"No, but…"

"Well, here's the deal, Christy. The only person you can change is yourself. You can't change Tom. You've tried everything under the sun, and nothing has worked. Your expectations have proved to be ineffective at motivating his behavior. If you keep expecting him to change to make you happy, you're going to continue to be disappointed and angry."

"I just want him to be a good provider like my father was."

"Yes, but your father was responsible and reliable. Tom isn't. Even though he's promised to change many times, he's proven over and over again that he's not committed to developing those character qualities."

I let out a huge sigh.

"So, since you can't change Tom, what can you do to change your thinking? If you change your expectations of Tom, you'll have a better chance of maintaining your own peace and sanity."

"I'm going to need some help with this one," I said.

"Let me walk you through this. You say that every time Tom promises that he's going to get up at a decent hour and go to work, you believe him, right?"

"Yes."

"And when he doesn't honor his promise, you fly off the handle."

"Yes."

"By believing a man who is unreliable, you're giving him control. He's controlling your peace. Proverbs says that relying on the unfaithful is like relying on a broken tooth or a lame foot. Your husband's actions have shown that he's not a man of his word."

"True."

"What if you could change your expectation to meet the reality of your situation? Then you wouldn't be tossed back and forth by your circumstances. If you don't expect him to be something he's not, you can have your peace back. If you have your peace back, you'll be in a better position to decide what to do. But if you're always angry, your anger will prevent peace and your ability to make wise choices."

"So you're saying, right now, I've given him control?"

"Exactly."

"Hmmm." I twirled a strand of hair.

"Let me ask you this. If your three-year-old daughter said she was going to paint the living room, would you give her the roller brush and paint?"

"Of course not. I'd only have a huge mess to clean up."

"So, consider this. If you *did* give her the roller brush and paint and expected her to do a good job, and then got angry when the can of paint spilled and ruined the carpet, whose fault would it be that you got angry—hers for making a mess or yours for having unrealistic expectations?"

"Oh, I think I see what you mean. Every time I hand over my expectations to Tom, he makes a huge mess that I end up having to clean."

"That's right! A husband *should* be reliable. But so far, Tom has proved that he's not. Expecting the unfaithful to honor their word is a set up for disappointment and anger. If you want to preserve your own peace of mind, you'll need to adjust your expectations."

REFRAMING EXPECTATIONS

In the months and years to come, I had plenty of opportunities to practice Barbara's advice. It wasn't easy. I likened it to learning to ride a bike. I needed training wheels at first. I called Barbara many times. She helped me look at each crisis from a different point of view and helped me adjust my expectations. In doing so, I learned that I could manage my own peace.

Eventually, like riding a bike, it got easier, and I was able to take off the training wheels. Even then, there were times I skinned my knees, but little by little, I reframed my expectations. It may have taken a lifetime to learn the bad habit of placing my trust in someone who was not trustworthy, but each situation gave me another chance to learn how to preserve my peace by changing my expectations.

When he was high or his actions were inappropriate, I reframed my thoughts. As I began to understand that his choices were not a reflection of my character, the shame slithered away.

If he was hostile and belligerent, I learned to protect my emotions by leaving the room or the premises if necessary. When he threatened physical harm, I filed a Victim's Protective Order. I wasn't going to wait until I had bruises to prove I'd been abused.

If he was out of work, instead of allowing myself to be consumed with worry, I asked God to help me renew my mind with His truth. He helped me dig up the roots of anger and fear and replace them with truth. God was my provider, not Tom. He would supply all of my needs, not Tom. In the past I'd placed all of my trust in Tom, but he was incapable of providing the security I needed. Each time he quit a job or got fired, I had another opportunity to ask God to help me reframe my thoughts.

When I was worried about a cut-off notice from my electric company or how I was going to pay for groceries, I reminded myself that I could choose panic or peace. Then I asked myself a few questions. *Did I have food to eat today? Were my utilities on today? Did I have gas in my car today?* These questions helped me refocus on my present situation instead of worrying about tomorrow and choose to praise God for what I had *today*.

When worries cropped back up, I reminded myself of His faithfulness in the past. Times like when our small group at church rallied together to provide our past due rent the day before our eviction notice would be served. Another time a friend who worked with a non-profit mentioned that we had nothing for Christmas. A knock on the door was an utter surprise when he brought over a turkey, bags of groceries, and toys for our two children…on Christmas Eve. These provisions helped me realize that, despite my husband's irresponsibility, God saw my needs. And as much as I wished that He didn't make me wait, He was always right on time.

WHERE IS THE HOLY SPIRIT IN ALL OF THIS CHAOS?

Focusing on His faithfulness also strengthened my confidence for the future. When fears resurfaced, I focused on scripture truths like:

- God shall supply all of my needs according to his riches in glory (Philippians 4:19).
- Today, I have everything I need for life and godliness (2 Peter 1:3).
- The Lord is my strength and my shield; my heart trusts in him, and I am helped (Psalm 28:7).

I decided that my focus would be on today—not tomorrow. Worrying about tomorrow was futile. Besides that, it destroyed my ability to enjoy today and the things in my life that were good now—my children, my friends, and my growing relationship with God.

Up until that point, getting a divorce or staying miserably married were the only two options I knew, but Barbara helped me discover other options. "If you're going to choose to stay in this marriage, you can remain resentful and angry, but you could also choose to maintain your own peace. So far, you've allowed him to control that, but you can take it back."

Christian counselor and relationship coach Leslie Vernick echoes this advice. In her book, *The Emotionally Destructive Marriage: How to Find Your Voice and Reclaim Your Hope*, she writes about what she calls staying well.

> If you are going to stay in this marriage, then stay well; and if you are going to leave your marriage, then leave well. In other words,

you are responsible for the person you are and are becoming in the fire of this difficult marriage. It is important to realize that you give God no glory, nor do your children any favors, if you stay married with a heart full of bitterness, resentment, fear, hatred, or indifference. God wants much more for you than that.[19]

I knew God had not released me from my marriage. I hoped and prayed He would restore it. Instead, He was using the difficulties in my marriage to free me from false beliefs that caused me to rely on my husband for peace and joy. As long as I was willing, He wanted to help me tear down the mindsets that prevented me from experiencing emotional freedom. Like a home that needed renovation, He was knocking down the studs of unrealistic expectations and destroying the disabling lies that told me my circumstances ruled my peace and that someone else was responsible for my happiness.

Abraham Lincoln is often quoted as having said, "Most folks are about as happy as they make up their mind to be."

As unpleasant as it was, each difficulty gave me another opportunity to learn how to redirect my thoughts and expectations. I was growing more peaceful and confident. I was learning the promise that the Apostle Paul talks about in Romans 5:

Suffering produces endurance.

Endurance produces character.

Character produces hope.

And hope does not put us to shame.

Friend, if unmet expectations have destroyed your peace, you too can change them. Take a moment to consider the expectations you have of your partner. Are they rigid and unrealistic? Do they rob your peace when they go unmet? Are you giving him control of your sanity? Even expectations of previous partners and spouses that you have failed to release are like bricks cemented in your soul.

An expectation is a hope. When we put all of our hope in our partner or spouse and they fail to meet our expectations, the end result is disappointment. The book of Psalms says that a horse is a vain hope for safety and deliverance; despite all its great strength it cannot save or rescue us (Psalms 33:17). Neither can our men. Shifting our hope and expectations to a secure source is a better option. Hear what the real promise of faithfulness is: "But the eyes of the Lord are on those who fear him, on those whose hope is in his unfailing love" (Psalm 33:18). Only God can deliver our soul from the death of dreams and unmet expectations.

Maybe you're thinking God has let you down as well. That's understandable. If nothing has turned out the way you've hoped, sometimes you may even feel that God has disappointed you. If that's you, let me say this: I understand. I once felt that way too. But, can I challenge you to keep reading? Like the teardown in a house remodel makes a gigantic mess, this first step of changing your expectations reveals a lot of emotional debris. But as you go through the next steps in rebuilding your castle, I hope you'll see that a new you is in your future. Hang in there, sister. In the next chapter, we're going to look at several false beliefs many of us have about forgiveness. I think you'll begin to see more hope as some of the emotional clutter is cleared out and taken to the dump.

PONDER AND PRACTICE

1. Like I once did with Tom, how have you allowed men to be

in charge of your own happiness?
2. What bricks from your past do you need to let go of?
3. Whether they are reasonable or not, unmet expectations are a down payment on resentment. If you want to preserve your own peace of mind and experience emotional freedom, what mindsets or expectations do you need to adjust?

- 14 -

THE LEVERAGE OF FORGIVENESS

I HATE YOU!" CHELSEA DECLARED one day in a fit of anger. The words slipped out of her mouth faster than a spit wad out of a straw. Unfortunately, they were the last words she ever spoke to her husband.

Chelsea didn't know Blake would die later that day in a four-wheeler accident. If she had, maybe she would've bit her tongue.

The angry outburst haunted her for years. Tormented by the anguish she feared would never be resolved, Chelsea spent many nights trying to swathe her sorrow. She believed a huge lie: forgiveness required a personal apology.

Like many women, Chelsea had a hard time releasing an offense when the offender was not available. When the men we're angry with are deceased, have disappeared, or for other reasons are unwilling to communicate, these final dialogues often echo in our mind. They ricochet back and forth while an invisible amplifier magnifies their volume.

They did for Peter after he denied Jesus. Imagine some of the last words Jesus spoke to Peter before his death. "This very night, before the rooster crows, you will disown me three times." (Matthew 26:34)."

"Never!" declared Peter. And yet, when he heard the rooster's crows, the sting of this unimaginable prediction pierced his heart.

Like a divine annulment, Peter was saying the love he felt for Christ never existed. And he didn't just claim that he didn't know Christ; Peter added some colorful dialogue that Matthew edited out of his gospel. In his manner-of-fact tone, Matthew said that Peter began to curse and swear saying, "I don't know the man!" And as soon as the dreadful words rolled off his tongue, with the precision of a dramatic Hollywood screenplay, immediately a rooster crowed. (Matthew 26:74).

Yes, Peter the apostle was a wimpy coward and yet, just ten chapters earlier, Christ said this to him: "And now I'm going to tell you who you are, really are. You are Peter, a rock" (Matthew 16:17, The Message).

It's hard to imagine, but here was a man whom Jesus said was so rock solid that he would build his church on the strength of his soul, and yet the same man was capable of denying *and* cursing his savior. And now, from across the courtyard, Peter's shame-filled eyes met the eyes of Christ. And with the guilt of a murder suspect caught with blood on his hands, the rock-solid disciple ran away.

Like Chelsea's final words to her husband, Peter's last words about someone he loved were an angry outburst.

A regretted curse.

A grave mistake.

Seeing Peter's faults offers me hope. It makes me realize just how imperfect the disciples were. They weren't superheroes. The men Jesus picked to be his closest companions were normal men—men who made mistakes, men who were prone to failure, and men who cowered under the pressure of fear. Men with inadequacies, just like us.

Thankfully, for every time we fail, God's mercy prevails. After his resurrection, Jesus asked Peter three times, "Peter, do you love me?" He didn't just ask him once. Jesus wanted to clear the slate. For each of the three times Peter denied knowing him, Jesus gave him an opportunity to make it right.

What about you? Have you ever cursed God or hurled angry words at someone you love? I know I have. More times than I care to admit.

I hate you!

You can't do anything right!

I want a divorce!

No matter how grave our mistakes, Jesus longs to remove the burden of our guilt. Christ saw Peter's future with telepathic vision. Looking past his denial, he saw the intended result of Peter's life, when the Christian Coward would morph into a solid-rock Guardian of Truth.

Christ sees your future, too. He sees past your riveting regrets and grave mistakes. If you've ever imagined that the disciples were perfect, Peter's story trashes that idea. Aren't you thankful that perfection is not a prerequisite for pardon? God chose me and you, despite our shortcomings. He calls forth character in us before it's developed. He loves us when we deny Him, curse others, or struggle to forgive. He sees past our failures and into our future. His grace covers our sins, and through His mercy, he reconciles our defeats. Like Peter, His grace makes us rock solid.

MALICIOUS MELODIES

Chelsea spent years in regret before she let go of her anguish. "It was hard because my husband wasn't here. I went to his grave and told him how sorry I was for my angry outburst, but I'd never hear his amends. Without closure, I fell into depression. I'd always believed that an apology was necessary in order for forgiveness to be extended. Obviously, I wasn't going to get one. Death didn't discharge the offense. But no matter if my husband was here or not, I needed to forgive so I could be free."

The need for vindication holds many of us captive to bitterness. When we are lied to, mistreated, or abused, we often hold onto our grudge until justice is served. In doing so, we sabotage our own freedom. Like Chelsea learned, however, an apology doesn't have to be communicated in person. We forgive from our heart.

Let's set the record straight with some other truths about forgiveness:

- Forgiveness doesn't mean the other person's actions were acceptable.
- When we forgive, we don't release the offender from the natural consequences of their actions or from the legal obligation for restitution.
- Forgiving is not something we do for the other person. We forgive so we can be free.
- Unforgiveness may or may not hurt the other person, but it always hurts us.
- Trust has to be earned.
- Forgiving someone doesn't mean you have to trust the offender again.

The Leverage of Forgiveness

- ✧ Forgiving doesn't mean you forget.
- ✧ Forgiveness doesn't require reconciliation.

"Today, I'm brutal about keeping bitterness out," Chelsea explained. The enemy uses the same ol' lies to deceive me, but I'm on to him now. I'm not going to let him take me down again."

Satan wants our forgiveness failures to haunt us. He magnifies every offense committed against us in hopes that we'll stay bitter. He keeps records of wrongs for us so we'll never walk in God's grace and abundance. Then he reminds us of all of our own trespasses against God to amplify our unworthiness. Even when we've worked through forgiveness, he'll try the same trick again. It worked before. Then he waits.

For an opportune time.

Patience, albeit the warped, twisted, and sneaky kind, is one quality Satan has perfected. He reasons that if we snapped at the bait of offense before, there's a good chance we'll fall for it again. That's why we have to be on guard.

"Be alert and of sober mind. Your enemy the devil prowls around like a roaring lion looking for someone to devour (I Peter 5:8)."

This is a common verse, one you've no doubt heard before. Even so, as a word nerd, I felt compelled to look up some meanings. I found it interesting that the Greek word for roaring, *ōryomai*, is only used *one* time in the entire Bible. One translation is obvious—to roar or howl. But another translation is peculiar: to sing with a loud voice. That got me thinking. It's easy to discern the enemy's voice when he roars or howls. We expect a lion or an enemy to be loud and scary. He's easy to recognize then. But, when he sings—that's a

Forgiving someone doesn't mean you have to *trust* the offender again. Trust has to be *earned.*

The Leverage of Forgiveness

different story. He catches us off guard. If he can woo us back into bitterness with malicious melodies wrapped in truth, he can take us hostage again.

Contrary to popular belief, Satan loves truth. He knows the Word of God inside and out. The very thing we love, he uses against us—by mixing it up. Changing one little detail. Then he uses his tangled version of truth as bait. But underneath the lure of the gospel is the hook of deceit. He uses a tagline of truism to draw us near to inspect and consider. If we appear to be cautious in pondering his perspective, he'll seduce us with more bait.

If the devil only spewed boldfaced lies, it'd be easy to recognize his deceit. But deception braided in truth is harder to detect.

THE FORGERY

Counterfeit causes and twisted tales are Satan's specialty. We wouldn't fall for something if it was all bad. He covers a lie with truth. The outside looks so good we won't take the time to analyze or inspect it until it's too late. Like a fish opening wide for the bait, we don't notice until we've been hooked. We fall for the lure, hook, line and sinker.

If the devil knows the truth, we have to know it too. And know it better.

In the late eighties, I worked as a bank examiner at the Tenth District Federal Reserve Bank in Kansas City. Part of my rookie duties involved conducting tours for banking groups, businesses, schools, and clubs, and anyone else who wanted to tour the exhibits that the bank had on the mezzanine level. Participants could see things like a high-speed sorter, which could sort more than one million checks a day, and the original vault, which had been built offsite for the bank. The door alone weighed thirty-five tons and the frame another fifteen tons. In September, 1921, it took a tractor, two five-ton trucks, and a team of four horses two days to haul the door and frame the ten blocks from the railroad yard to the bank. Ok, enough history. (Yes, I enjoyed giving those tours.)

By far, the most interesting exhibit for the participants was the counterfeit bill exhibit. This display consisted of one authentic bill and one counterfeit bill of each denomination under a large magnifying glass. Visitors gathered around the display to check out the bills and try to guess which ones were real. They'd always give detailed reasons why they were certain they'd picked the authentic bill, going into detail to support their opinion.

Most of the time, their answer would be something like, "Well, it *looks* like this bill is the fake one. See how the ink is smeared." Or, "It *looks* like this is the real bill because this seal is centered just right." Almost without exception, their answers were based on looks or appearances, not on factual information. They'd spend most of their time focusing on what they perceived to be as flaws on the bill and used those flaws to make their conclusion.

After they'd had their fun trying to guess which bills were authentic, I'd explain that FBI agents go through intensive training to be able to spot counterfeit bills. They're trained with such precision that they can spot a counterfeit at first glance. Eyes would bulge in astonishment. But then I'd blow them away with an even more startling fact—FBI agents never see a counterfeit bill during their training! Instead, they only study the real deal. They know it inside and out. Every detail, every symbol, and the purpose for every number printed on the bill.

If an FBI agent never saw a counterfeit, how could they tell the difference between the authentic and the fake? Simple. Knowing every detail of the genuine article made the forgery stand out.

The truth does set us free. Isn't this how you want to be? If you know the Bible well, when the enemy throws his version of truth at you, you'll be able to spot his deception without hesitation. If your mind is renewed and you've studied the truth, you'll be able to discern between what is real and what is fake. You'll not be taken captive through the hollow and deceptive philosophy that depends on human tradition and the basic principles of this world (Colossians 2:8).

BITTERNESS BLOCKS OUR ABILITY TO HEAR GOD

One of the greatest deceptions about unforgiveness is that it doesn't hurt us. Nothing could be further from the truth. Trudi's story is a profound example of this misconception.

"One of my friends had hurt me terribly, and I was having a hard time forgiving her," recalls Trudi. "It didn't help that one day I went to church and heard a message about forgiveness."

Isn't that how God is? Whenever we're struggling with something, we can't escape His reproof.

"I kept hearing the Holy Spirit say, 'You need to forgive her. You need to let this go.' Despite His urging, I wrestled with the offense and held on for several more days. Finally, I couldn't take it anymore. I got down on my knees one morning and prayed a short and simple prayer. 'Lord, forgive me for harboring this unforgiveness. I don't know how to let it go, but please, help me forgive her."

Later that evening, Trudi drew her four-year-old daughter a bath. While Brooke was playing with her toys in the tub, Trudi went into the kitchen to straighten up a few things. As she was putting some dishes away, she felt a twinge of panic creep up her spine.

"I felt a sudden urge that I needed to check on Brooke," said Trudi.

She ran to the bathroom, and, when she got there, Trudi not only found her daughter in the bathtub, but also her one-year-old baby, who had toddled in to see his sister and fallen in. Joshua's eyes were red and dripping with water. Bubbles covered the top of his head. Yet, to her surprise, he was sitting up.

She grabbed her baby in her arms, crying with relief that he was okay.

Brooke, noticing her mother's alarm, looked up with calm reassurance and said, "Mama, someone sat him up."

Of course, no one else was there.

That night, Trudi held her baby tight as she rocked him to sleep, praising God that Joshua didn't drown, praising God for His faithfulness. As she laid Joshua in his crib for the night, she felt the Lord's presence in the room. Trudi inhaled a deep breath and paused to listen. As she admired her sleeping baby, she sensed the Lord say, "If you hadn't forgiven, you may not have heard My voice today."

Bitterness is a blocker. It blocks our joy. It blocks the presence of God. And it blocks our ability to hear God's voice. Trudi's story is a powerful example of Isaiah's warning:

"But your iniquities have separated you from your God; your sins have hidden his face from you, so that he will not hear" (Isaiah 59:2).

I don't know what you're holding onto today, but harboring

bitterness is not worth the cost. You can't afford to be separated from God. Bitterness opens doors and opportunities for the enemy to waltz in and bring destruction. Trudi's simple prayer shows how easy forgiveness can be. When we admit that we don't know how to let go, all we need to do is ask for His help.

BITTERNESS DESTROYS OUR JOY

Desiree's parents were strict. They were all about appearances. Her father was a deacon in church, and her mother taught Sunday school. "If I ever complained or got mad," Desiree said, "my mom gave me a lecture about how I shouldn't feel that way. That I had so much to be grateful for. That's when I started stuffing my feelings. I learned to be oblivious to my emotions and how I felt. My upbringing taught me to perform to certain standards. Ladies behave. They don't yell. It was never spoken, but the message I heard was that it was wrong to feel anger."

Anger has to go somewhere. If we don't acknowledge it and release it to God, it goes inward, into a place like an invisible container that grows toxic mold and mildew on the walls of our soul.

That's the way bitterness works, too. It poisons our own body and it robs us of our ability to experience joy. Think about it. Have you ever met any angry happy people? They may look happy on the outside, concealing their anger with a smile and kind words. They may've even convinced themselves that they aren't angry.

"When I got married, I never voiced my displeasure about anything Devin did," said Desiree. "I'd denied my feelings for so long, I couldn't recognize them. I was miserable and knew something was wrong, but I didn't know what. One day I was reading in Psalms and saw a passage that shocked me. David poured out his complaints to God. *Wow,* I thought. *God didn't strike him dead? Instead, He listened?* Until then, I had no idea it was okay to tell God how I felt. I'd never cried so much in my life as I did that day. But afterward, I felt such a relief. I felt my joy return. I guess David's did, too. The last verse of that chapter said, 'Bring my soul out of prison, that I may praise thy name.'"

Desiree's story is not uncommon. When we stuff our pain and anger and try to cover it up to please others or present an image that we want others to believe, we lose ourselves in the process. Stuffing feelings is never a good option. Tell God how you feel. He wants to dialogue with you. He created you to be able to feel emotions, but He doesn't want you to be trapped in despair and bitterness. When you pour out your complaints to Him, He is able to restore your soul.

ANGER IS PROGRESSIVE

Anger is progressive, and it has to go somewhere. As it grows, it either implodes and goes inside or it explodes in an outburst or a fit of rage. Either way, anger not released in forgiveness grows into bitterness and resentment. As it develops further, it turns into vengeance, apathy, depression, or maybe even into suicidal or homicidal thoughts.

Some women *know* they're angry and have no trouble expressing it. For the record, this used to be my anger personality. Other women handle anger another way—they bury it. Like Desiree, some have stuffed it for so long, they can't recognize it.

If you can relate to Desiree's story and wonder if you've buried your own anger, consider the following list. Check the statements that apply to you.

- ○ I'm afraid to disagree or express my opinion to my partner
- ○ I'd rather deny my feelings than deal with conflict
- ○ I've quit trying to express my opinion because he won't listen anyway
- ○ I allow my partner to dominate the conversation
- ○ I don't think it's polite to express a different opinion
- ○ I often feel taken advantage of
- ○ I give up in disagreements because I'm afraid of the conflict it'll bring
- ○ I'm afraid of rejection
- ○ I typically deny anything is wrong
- ○ I think that harmony means I should give in
- ○ I think confrontation is wrong

Take note of the statements you checked. Next we'll unveil some scripture truths that can help you change these false beliefs and release resentments.

TRUTH IS THE ANSWER

In the previous chapters, we inspected our castle to make sure that our windows and doors were fully functioning, and that our moat and chandeliers were operating. All of these parts of our castle are essential, but none of these elements can stand without the support of God's word and His truth. God's truth holds everything together and supports every facet of our dwelling. When I started writing

God created you to be able to feel *emotions* but He doesn't want you to be *trapped* in despair and bitterness.

this chapter, however, I was at a loss for what I'd use to illustrate this concept. So I went to google and looked at some diagrams. That's where I learned a new word—buttress.

Now, maybe you're smarter than I am, and you already know what a buttress is, but just in case, let me explain. A buttress is an architectural structure built against the wall of the castle that adds stability to reinforce the framework. It's an external prop that gives extra support and strength. For instance, when we feel like giving in to resentment, God's word acts like a buttress. It gives us the leverage to stand. His truth reinforces our ability to overlook offenses.

I don't know if you're a glass-half-full or a glass-half-empty gal, but in the list below I've noted several scriptures on bitterness along with its horrible side effects. Then I listed the opposites as forgiveness benefits. Here's the rundown:

Bitterness leads to evil. It's poisonous and destroys our health. It prevents us from hearing God's voice, and it's contagious. You've heard that misery loves company. So does bitterness. It makes us captive to sin. It's a depressant, makes us fools, hardens our hearts, leads to addiction, and brings judgment against us. It blocks God's forgiveness toward us and gives the devil a foothold in our lives.

Forgiveness, on the other hand, is amazing. It brings life and leads to righteousness. It acts like a medicine, brings health to our bodies and unites us to God. Forgiveness is contagious and sets us free. It's an anti-depressant and makes us wise. It softens our hearts, destroys lust, gives us compassion, allows God to forgive us, and keeps the devil away.

You might be more motivated to avoid the side effects, or you might be more inclined to get the benefits. Either way, it doesn't matter. I hope some of these buttress truths convince you once and for all that bitterness has to go!

Refrain from anger and turn from wrath; do not fret—it leads only to evil (Psalm 37:8).
- ◇ Bitterness leads to evil.
- ◇ Forgiveness leads to righteousness.

Make sure there is no root among you that produces such bitter poison (Deuteronomy 29:18).
- ◇ Bitterness is poisonous.
- ◇ Forgiveness acts like a medicine and feeds the soul with gratitude.

A tranquil heart is life to the body, But passion [envy, jealousy, anger] is rottenness to the bones (Proverbs 14:30 NASB).
- ◇ Bitterness destroys our health.
- ◇ Forgiveness brings health to our body.

But your iniquities have separated you from your God; your sins have hidden his face from you, so that he will not hear (Isaiah 59:2).
- ◇ Bitterness prevents us from hearing God's voice.
- ◇ Forgiveness unites us to God.

See to it that no one falls short of the grace of God and that no bitter root grows up to cause trouble and defile many (Hebrews 12:15).
- ◇ Bitterness is contagious.
- ◇ Forgiveness is also contagious.

For I see that you are full of bitterness and captive to sin (Acts 8:23).
- Bitterness creates a stronghold and makes us a slave.
- Forgiveness sets us free.

Another dies in bitterness of soul, never having enjoyed anything good (Job 21:25).
- Bitterness acts as a depressant.
- Forgiveness acts as an anti-depressant and multiplies joy.

Do not be quickly provoked in your spirit, for anger resides in the lap of fools (Ecclesiastes 7:9).
- Bitterness makes us fools.
- Forgiveness makes us wise.

They are darkened in their understanding and separated from the life of God because of the ignorance that is in them due to the hardening of their hearts (Ephesians 4:18).
- Bitterness hardens our heart.
- Forgiveness softens our heart.

Having lost all sensitivity, they have given themselves over to sensuality so as to indulge in every kind of impurity, and they are full of greed (Ephesians 4:19).
- Bitterness leads to addiction (yes, unhealthy relationships are a love addiction).
- Forgiveness destroys lust.

For *in the same way you judge others, you will be judged* (Matthew 7:2).
- ✧ Bitterness brings judgment against us.
- ✧ Forgiveness gives us compassion.

But if you do not forgive others their sins, your Father will not forgive your sins (Matthew 6:15).
- ✧ Bitterness blocks God's forgiveness to us.
- ✧ Bitterness allows God to forgive us.

In *your anger do not sin. Do not let the sun go down while you are still angry, and do not give the devil a foothold* (Ephesians 4:26-27).
- ✧ Bitterness gives the devil a foothold.
- ✧ Forgiveness keeps the devil away.

PONDER AND PRACTICE

1. Which side effects of bitterness are most alarming to you?
2. Which benefits of forgiveness do you need the most?
3. Look over the list of scriptures. Which ones need your attention the most?

- 15 -

THE VIEW FROM THE WATCHTOWER

JOSEPH'S LIFE BEGAN IN prosperity and partiality. As his father's favorite child, I think he probably had TPS—teacher's pet syndrome. If you've ever been a teacher's favorite, you may have noticed—the only one who likes you…

is the teacher.

Kids probably made fun of you behind your back. They may have even plotted your assassination on the playground. Joseph's dad didn't hide his favoritism. He gave him a coat of many colors, a distinguishing gift that set him apart and Joseph wore it proudly like a letterman's jacket.

Favor is a gift from God, but if not controlled, it morphs into pride. And pride often comes standard with a few accessories like tattling and boasting. Traits that made Joseph's brothers despise him. His story begins in the thirty-seventh chapter of Genesis. Once, when he was tending the flocks with his brothers, he brought his father a bad report about them. Making others look bad so you look good doesn't usually play out well.

Shortly after, he had a dream that he broadcasted to his brothers. "We were binding sheaves of grain out in the field when suddenly my sheaf rose and stood upright, while your sheaves gathered around mine and bowed down to it."

Big mistake.

His brothers weren't so fond of his vision. In fact, they despised him so much they wanted him dead. One day while they were all out in the field together, they saw Joseph coming in the distance and started plotting to kill him. When he arrived they threw him in a cistern and sat down to eat lunch to talk about how they were going to pull off his murder.

Instead, they saw a caravan of Ishmaelites on their way to Egypt and thought they might make some money on the deal by selling him as a slave.

Joseph garnered twenty shekels. #HumanTrafficking

But first they stole his robe.

The richly ornamented coat given to him by his father represented Joseph's status, his future, and his destiny. His brothers got hand-me-downs from the thrift store, but Joseph's coat came from Saks Fifth Avenue. His hand-tailored coat was made of the finest wool and dyed with colors that distinguished him as royalty. It was a visible sign that advertised he was the chosen one, destined for greatness and set apart for fortune and fame. Success was sewn between each seam. His coat embodied his identity and future.

But now, not only was Joseph a victim of attempted murder and human trafficking, a reject plucked from his home and family, but his identity had been stolen as well.

Most people would want to give up. Many would be angry with God. Others would withdraw, abandon hope and give up on their dreams—but not Joseph. He waited on the Lord, and God caused favor to rest on him. He was placed in the house of Potiphar, one of Pharaoh's officials, as an overseer. The Lord was with Joseph, and he prospered.

Even in bondage, God's hand was upon Joseph.

But again, someone tried to strip him of his honor. When Joseph refused the sexual advances of Potiphar's wife, she stole his robe and accused him of rape.

What is it about Joseph and his robe? Now, he's a two-time loser. His robe was stolen twice, and, both times, false accusations were made against him. His brothers lied to his father: "Dad, here's Joseph's coat. He's been eaten by a wild animal." Potiphar's wife lied to her husband: "That slave you brought in here tried to rape me." Both used his garment to prove their allegations. The very thing God used to set Joseph apart was the thing that others scorned.

Next, Joseph was thrown in prison. His problems were just beginning, but his issues didn't take him down. Joseph prospered even in prison. The Bible says that the Lord was with Joseph.

I believe God gave Joseph a dream when he was a young man to motivate his endurance. Twenty-two years of hardship needed a vision.

At seventeen, Joseph wasn't ready to lead. God knew the road ahead, and He knew Joseph would need some reassurance that adversity was preparing him for his future. Joseph was the favorite, but that didn't make him qualified. Endurance would qualify him.

You may not be in prison, but the Lord is with you, too. God is with you when you are suffering. He is with you when your husband has an affair or wants a divorce. He is with you when your fiancé calls the wedding off at the last minute. God is with you when addiction tries to destroy your life or when you've been a victim of control, manipulation, or abuse.

Thankfully, the book of 1 Peter tells us that there's an end to our suffering. Joseph's hardship finally halted when Pharaoh recognized his wisdom. Joseph was released from prison, and, in one day, his destiny changed forever. Pharaoh dressed Joseph in a robe of fine linen and put a gold chain around his neck. Joseph rode in a chariot as second-in-command as men shouted before him, "Make way!"

In one day, Joseph went from prison to power. In one day, he went from a convict to a commander. And in one day, Joseph got his robe back.

Has your robe been stolen? Has someone trampled on your destiny and tried to squelch your future? No one can steal a God-given dream. Joseph got his robe back…and so will you!

BETWEEN THE DREAM AND THE DESTINY

Joseph was a young man of seventeen when God gave him his dream that one day his family would bow down to him. Immediately after his divine vision, however, he was slammed with adversity as his brothers sold him into slavery. There's some true family unity for you. And you thought *All My Children* was a dramatic soap opera. His brothers pocketed twenty shekels. Hmm. Jesus went for thirty gold coins. I guess inflation existed even back then.

Did you notice what happened right after Joseph's dream? Difficulties.

Often a dream is a ticket into the desert.

Many years ago, I had a dream to write. Did you notice I said *many years*? For some reason, I thought it was going to happen overnight. I'm not sure I ever would have started if I had known how long God intended to draw the process out. Joseph must have felt the same way about his dream. Plus, his situation got much worse before it got better. After thirteen years of slavery and prison, Joseph could have given up. But he never let go of his vision.

God had a plan all along to restore Joseph's life. At thirty years old, Joseph's life changed dramatically when he interpreted a dream and entered the service of Pharaoh, king of Egypt. After all he had endured, don't you know he must have been tempted to think, *If only my brothers could see me now. Surely it's only a matter of minutes before my dream will completely manifest.*

But even after Joseph became second in command, it was still another nine years before he was reunited with his brothers.

As he had predicted with Pharaoh's dream, Egypt experienced seven years of abundance before the world famine began. Because he instructed Pharaoh to store up grain, when the famine began, other countries eventually came to Egypt to buy grain. Months passed before his family was desperate enough for food to travel to Egypt.

Why do you think the Bible points out this detailed timeline? I think Joseph's not so fast track to success can encourage us when we think we have suffered long enough. If Joseph could endure years of hardship, I can press on when my issues linger.

Twenty-two years is a long time to wait on a dream. But God was with Joseph in times of attempted murder, adversity, imprisonment, and false accusation. Maybe your dream is for your marriage to be restored or for the right man to come along. Maybe you've been waiting for a long time. If you've endured abuse, rejection, or sorrow, the Lord is with you, too. He is with you in trouble. He's not forgotten you. Even in the midst of your trials and tears, He is mindful of your situation. He's not left you. He's working out His plan.

The day Joseph saw his brothers bow before him in request for food must have been a surreal day. It probably wasn't hard to recognize them in their traditional Hebrew dress, but they didn't have a clue who he was. For one thing, Joseph looked different in his Egyptian wig and makeup. Besides, they could never have imagined that the brother they sold as a slave would now be in command.

Genesis 42 tells us that ten of Joseph's brothers went down to buy grain from Egypt. As they bowed low before him with their faces to the ground, somehow Joseph knew it wasn't time to reveal himself.

Joseph's situation reminds me of delivering my first child—without an epidural, I might add. I had spent several hours at the hospital when the doctor sent me home because I wasn't dilating. By the time my mucus plug broke and my husband brought me back to the hospital, there was no time for pain relief. While natural childbirth was not my original choice—even though I thought I had a high tolerance to pain—I soon discovered that slamming my finger in a window doesn't even register on the pain Richter scale. The pain of childbirth was a ten, and I thought I was about to die. Just when Brittany was crowning, the doctor yelled, "Don't push yet. Hold off. Wait a minute."

Excuse me? Did someone notice I'm about to flat line?

With the amount of restraint it would take to hold back a volcanic eruption, I forced my body to comply. Somehow, I had to trust that the doctor knew the perfect time, and I managed to tell myself, *Focus. Focus. Don't push yet. Wait just another minute.*

Joseph had to wait, too.

The opportunity he had anticipated for over two decades was before him, and yet, somehow he knew it wasn't the right time.

The View From the Watchtower

How did he know? And how was he able to restrain himself?

Let's check out his dream again. In Genesis 37, Joseph told his brothers, "I had another dream, and this time the sun and moon and eleven stars were bowing down to me."

As Joseph watched his clueless brothers bowing before him, maybe he remembered that there had been eleven stars in his dream, not ten. A brother was missing. Chills must have swept over him as he realized his youngest brother was missing.

Even though Joseph waited for over twenty-two years to see his promise fulfilled, he didn't settle for the first apparent fulfillment of his dream. This wasn't the right time to reveal his identity. Instead, he showed restraint and patience. Years of adversity had produced patience and longsuffering.

It may have seemed like Joseph's reaction to his brothers was harsh when he accused them of being spies, but this was all a divine plot twist to get his brothers to go home and return to Egypt with his younger brother.

So again, Joseph waited. Waiting was the story of his life, but this time Joseph knew the promise was closer than ever. The next several months must have been pure torture. Often the closer we get to our promise, the harder the waiting is to endure.

By the time his older brothers returned with his younger brother in Genesis 45, Joseph could no longer contain himself. He asked all his attendants to leave and wept so loudly the Egyptians heard him. Then he called his brothers close and said, "Look at me! I am your brother Joseph, the one you sold into slavery."

His brothers were terrified and speechless. Surely they were dead meat. He had the power to kill them or put them in prison.

But adversity matured Joseph. By now, he understood the purpose in his pain. He saw his circumstances from a different vantage point—a higher view. Joseph was able to overlook the trespasses committed against him because he was able to see his situation from a kingdom perspective. Joseph climbed up to his watchtower.

THE LOOKOUT POINT

A watchtower is the lookout point on the castle. From that vantage point, we can see our enemies approach from a long distance away. We can prepare for assaults and plan our counterattack. From this viewpoint we have a better chance of seeing our circumstances from God's perspective. Habakkuk wrote: "I will climb up to my watchtower and stand at my guardpost. There I will wait to see what the Lord says and how he will answer my complaint" (Habakkuk 2:1 NLT).

The Lord speaks when we climb up to our watchtower. Joseph saw his betrayal, the false accusations, and his slavery and imprisonment from a different perspective. He understood that his brothers' rejection started him on a path ordained by God to deliver him to his destiny—and to deliver the known world from starvation. His brothers ultimately bowed before him, but Joseph bowed first. He submitted to the plan of God. He endured and received his promise.

In Genesis 45:5 Joseph exposes his heart with one of the most piercing forgiveness statements I've ever heard. Listen to what he says to his brothers, who are trembling in fear. "Do not be distressed and do not be angry with yourselves for selling me here, because it was to save lives that God sent me ahead of you."

EAGLE EYES OR BUMBLE BEES

As believers, we have two different ways of looking at our circumstances. We can view our world through the lens of our physical reality, or we can climb up to our watchtowers to see things through the lens of our spiritual reality—God's perspective.

I love how God showcases His truth in nature. We can see these principles operating in the lives of bees and eagles. Author Ann Lamott said this in her Ted Talk, *12 Truths I Learned from Life and Writing*. "My pastor said you can trap bees on the bottom of mason jars without lids because they don't look up, so they just walk around bitterly bumping into the glass walls. Go outside. Look up. Secret of life."[20]

Sometimes we're like bees. We stay trapped in despair and misery even though there's nothing blocking our freedom except our own refusal to look up. We never see heaven's agenda or the kingdom forecast. Instead, we stay bound in bitterness. Since you have the Holy Spirit living on the inside of you, however, you have the capacity to see through His eyes.

Eagles can see things from two different focal points at the same time. Their eyes have two foveae, which allow them to see straight ahead as well as view objects from a sideways vantage point long distances away. In fact, an eagle can see a rabbit more than three miles away.

In a similar way, when you view your circumstances from your watchtower, you can see things that are impossible to observe at ground level. Dear sister, there's always a promise beyond the pain. It's time to climb up to your watchtower. God wants to show you great and mighty things.

PAIN PRECEDES CHILDBIRTH

What if a woman didn't realize that she was nine months pregnant? What if she thought that she had gained weight for no legitimate reason? What if she started labor and didn't realize that she was in the midst of birthing a baby? This sounds ridiculous because it's hard to imagine that a woman wouldn't realize she was pregnant. But if she weren't aware of the process, she'd no doubt assume by the measure of pain that she was dying!

On the other hand, a woman who understands what is involved in pregnancy and childbirth is prepared for the pain. But she is willing to endure the pain because of the hope that is waiting on the other side of her suffering. She knows the fruit of her pain will be a precious baby.

She's informed of the process. Countless women before her have endured the same pain. There are books and doctors and videos that all advise exactly what to expect.

She knows she may live near a toilet for the first several months, consume large quantities of crazy cuisine, waddle like a duck, and have more mood swings than a schizophrenic kangaroo, but she knows she'll make it. It may seem like an eternity, but it won't last forever.

She understands her suffering has a season. There is an end. If she has morning sickness, tender breasts, food cravings, swollen feet, frequent urges for the nearest bathroom, at least she has comfort in knowing that in nine months, it'll be over. And there'll be a precious child.

Likewise, there is a promise of glory on the other side of our pain.

In the same way that a mother endures the pain because of the joy set before her, we can endure our troubles if we can get God's perspective on our pain, that at the end of our travail, He has a beautiful treasure in store for us. When we fix our eyes on Him, we can capture the promise of 2 Corinthians 4:17—our light and momentary troubles are achieving for us an eternal glory that far outweighs them all.

So what's on the other side of your pain? Climb up to your watchtower and ask God to give you a glimpse. Don't stay trapped in your bitterness. God wants your focus to be centered on Him. Like a woman in childbirth, ask Him for a focal point. Rest assured, it won't be the pain. He wants to reveal the gain, the prize, the treasure, the thing He wants to birth and bring forth out of your pain.

Because suffering has a purpose.

WHEN THE LIGHT SHINES BRIGHT

Permanent change rarely comes without the perspective of revelation. When God reveals His truth to us, we're changed from the inside out as He causes us to see our circumstances through His eyes. If we only see our life through the lens of our physical reality, we're only seeing half of the picture. It's like seeing the wrong side of a quilt before the lining is attached. We see a tangled mess of knots and loose threads from all the squares of fabric sewn together. But God wants us to see the finished side where all the colors merge together in glory.

Despite being betrayed by his own brothers, sold into slavery, falsely accused of rape, and thrown into prison, Joseph recognized that God meant it all for good—for the saving of men's lives. I'm sure in the middle of his mess, he fought despair and struggled with anger. He must have been tempted like we all are, but through his trials, he chose to trust God in spite of his hardships. In the end, sitting on his throne ruling Egypt, he saw his situation through God's eyes.

Queen Esther was another person who faced life-threatening challenges. The book of Esther tells the story of her bravery. When the king signed an edict into law to kill the entire Jewish nation, Esther was faced with a dangerous dilemma. The king didn't know she was a Jew, and if she approached him to appeal his decision, she could be put to death. In spite of the risk, Esther trusted God. There was an entire nation on the line. Esther saw God's purpose in her pain and was willing to obey, even if it meant that she perished.

Jesus knew his death on the cross would produce life because he saw the victory on the other side of his circumstances. He saw God's purpose in his pain.

God meant to produce freedom from my story, too. He is still using every shard of sorrow to bring Him glory. Today, I'm grateful for every fight and every conflict I'd ever had with Tom. Without the pain, I would never have been so desperate to lean into God. And if I'd never learned how to lean into God and trust Him for an answer, I'd never have been desperate enough to learn how to live in forgiveness and the freedom it brings. I would have lived in the dungeon of despair instead of winning from the watchtower.

My exasperation produced desperation.

And my desperation produced deliverance.

That's His specialty. Hope from hurt. Beauty from ashes. Purpose from pain.

My exasperation **produced** desperation. And my desperation produced **deliverance.**

PONDER AND PRACTICE

Now it's your turn. I want you to ask God what He's doing in your situation. Beg him for an answer. There's space on the next page where you can write down what He says, or you can use your own journal. Please don't skip this step!

After Habakkuk climbed into his watchtower and inquired of the Lord, the Lord told him to write the vision down, to make it plain on tablets (Habakkuk 2:2). That's what you need to do also. Without vision, you'll perish in your pain. If you don't do it now, find time in the next couple of days to get into His presence and ask Him to reveal his purpose in your situation.

When you partner with God, He can accomplish His purpose in your life. If you never see your situation through the light of what He wants to do, however, you'll linger in misunderstanding and misery. Satan will twist every detail into a dump of despair and you'll only see things from the side of your earthly kingdom.

But when you turn on the lights in your castle and invite the presence of the Holy Spirit inside, you'll see things you've never seen before. You'll be driven to the watchtower because you long to see even more. When you comprehend what God is doing in the midst of your difficulties, He'll bring hope beyond your suffering and allow you to see the glory beyond the now.

And it's always more beautiful than you could ever imagine.

So go ahead. Write the vision down. Make it plain.

To remind yourself. . .
To keep your focus. . .
To bring God glory!

The View From the Watchtower

Here are some questions you may want to use to get started:

- » God, what are you doing in my situation?
- » How can I see my circumstances from Your perspective?
- » Where have I seen pain when You see purpose?
- » What scriptures or promises do You want me to hang on to?

- 16 -

DIVINE WHISPERS

IN SEPTEMBER OF 1993, I signed up for a Bible study, *Communicating with God*. Until this point in my life, my conversations with God were pure monologues. I was intrigued to learn that God wanted to speak back to me. One of the first assignments was a journaling exercise. I had never journaled in my life, and to be honest, I doubted my ability to hear God that way. I didn't understand how I could distinguish between God's voice and my own imagination. I completed the exercise anyway. That's when God first spoke to me about Jake.

I am going to give you a son in December, and you are to name him Jacob because he will be a forerunner.

Those words squashed me like an elephant on an ant pile. Having another child in the middle of marital and financial difficulties was the furthest thing from my mind. Like the mature Christian that I was, I responded with an attitude of deep submission. I told God flat out that I wasn't going to cooperate. "I've heard you're quite good in the immaculate conception department. If this is really Your plan, You don't need my help!"

I started birth control measures at once. If I was going to have a baby in December, as far as I was concerned, nine months prior, I planned to have a long-term headache.

Even though I had effective strategies in motion, I wasn't convinced that I'd heard the actual voice of God. The greater possibility was that my own mind was playing tricks. After all, this had been my first attempt at hearing God's voice.

In order to verify my doubts, I decided to do some research to find out what the name Jacob meant. In 1993 the internet wasn't accessible to the general public, so a trip to the library was necessary. I found the section that had books for baby names and their meanings. I selected a book off the shelf and turned to the J's. There is was. Half way down the page.

Jacob. Hebrew origin. Meaning: deceiver, cheater.

Gee. Thanks God. You told me to name my son a deceiver? That's awfully spiritual of You!

For a moment I thought I was off the hook. A forerunner was not a deceiver. A forerunner was someone who goes ahead. A forerunner was someone who paves the way and prepares a way for others to follow. Like John the Baptist. John wasn't a deceiver.

But just to be sure, I wanted one more book to confirm my suspicions that I'd made this whole Jacob thing up.

I grabbed another baby name book off the shelf and flipped to the J's.

Jacob. *pronunciation:* JAY-kub. Meaning: *One who gets ahead by an unfair advantage.*

A chill traveled up my spine.

My long-term headache would start in March.

Just to be sure.

When April passed and I wasn't pregnant, I thought I was off the hook. But God is good at getting His way. When He said He was giving me a baby in December, I assumed that meant I would deliver in December.

Wrong.

I conceived in December. My headache was over by then.

When I discovered that I was pregnant, I *knew* it was a boy. I didn't need to see the results of the ultrasound. That's why it surprised me so much when one day during my early pregnancy with Jake, God told me something else.

I was out running some errands and pulled up to a stoplight at the intersection of Memorial and Bryant in Edmond, Oklahoma. When God speaks, you may not be able to explain it, but you just *know*. Your friends may think you're crazy, but you have this undeniable, never-forget-where-you-were experience. That's when I heard a divine whisper.

Sierra.

It was as if God's spirit swept in through a crack in the window, settled into the passenger seat, and engulfed me with His presence. I call it a divine whisper because I don't know how else to describe it. I didn't hear a voice, but the encounter left me with a sudden awareness—an unshakable impression that something vital to Jacob's future was wrapped in the meaning of Sierra.

Today, the name Sierra is common, but back in 1995, I had never heard it before. Sierra sounded like a girl's name to me, so at first, I thought I must be having twins. That seemed to fit with the name that God had given me for Jake, because the Jacob in the Bible was a twin. So I asked my doctor on my next visit about the possibility of having twins. She assured me there was only one heartbeat, but I wasn't convinced.

I'd heard stories about women who were only expecting a single birth and were surprised when they delivered twins. The other baby had gone undetected during ultrasounds because one twin was hiding behind the other. This only intensified my concerns. When I was seven months along and going on vacation, the flight attendants on the airplane questioned whether or not I should be flying. Many asked me if I was having twins. I was huge.

My doctor is a smart lady, but education and degrees don't always explain the divine. I am semi-smart myself, but the mystery of Sierra reduced me to stupid. After I had delivered Jake, I wiggled my finger and motioned the nurse to come close. "Are you sure that there's not another baby in there?"

"No, honey, we're all done." She laughed.

No closer to solving the mystery, I wondered if I was supposed to have another baby. But ten months after Jake was born, my husband and I divorced. Being a single mother with three children in my late thirties was hardly a good recipe for another child. Now it seemed doubtful that another child could be in my future.

A couple of years after my divorce, I met John. At this point in my life, having another child was the last thing I wanted, but after he proposed, I was desperate to get to the bottom of my Sierra charade. One day I started digging for clues.

"If you could have another child," I began, "and it was a girl… what would you name her?"

Without hesitation, John blurted out, "Sarah!"

It was almost a bulls-eye, but close doesn't get a cigar. I explained to John why I'd asked him. We were both amazed about the similarities, but I still wasn't any closer to solving the puzzle.

It was as if God's spirit *swept* in through a crack in the window, settled into the passenger seat, and *engulfed* me with His presence.

APRIL 23, 1998

I admired John's walk with the Lord and knew he would make a wonderful husband. One day he asked if I would join him in a day of prayer and fasting. It sounded like a spiritual thing to do, but in all honesty, the prayer and fasting combo has never been my jam. Since I'm rather fond of mealtime, my favorite prayer has always been grace. But John wanted us to pray and fast for unity in our future marriage. How could I say no to that?

It was a Thursday. I came home on my lunch hour and, during my prayer time, I felt God lead me to pick up a pen and start writing. Never mind that I was praying for my upcoming marriage. But as God would have it, He had other things to say. Out of the blue, this thought suffused my spirit. *Sierra means in the presence of God.* I didn't understand why He was telling me now what Sierra meant, but I wrote it down. Confused, I closed my journal and headed back to work.

Later that night John called. "Guess what?"

"What?" said John.

"God told me what Sierra means today."

"Really!" John's voice was high pitched, and he sounded far more excited than I thought the situation warranted. "What did He tell you?"

"When I was journaling, I felt like I heard him say, 'Sierra means in the presence of God.'"

"That. Is. A-mazing!" John exclaimed.

I let out a big sigh. "Not really...it's just a *meaning*. I still don't know the *why*. It's so frustrating."

"Well, you're not going to believe this, but the same thing happened to me."

"What do you mean?"

"God told me the same thing! I've never journaled before today, but…I'm looking at my notebook right now and here it is, in writing. *Sierra means in God's presence.*"

I was blown away. The fact that God included John in this game of synchronized secrets made me realize that the mystery of Sierra was more significant than I'd realized.

Without a doubt, I experienced the power of fasting in unified prayer that day. I still didn't have a clue why God whispered the name Sierra to me when I was pregnant with Jake, but it wouldn't be much longer. God was depositing a treasure in advance, preparing me for a day when I needed to hear His voice the most.

Six weeks later.

GOD'S WHISPERS REVEALED

The news of Jake and Garrett's car accident threatened to paralyze me. After my talk with Officer Harp, Officer George, and Dr. Mantor, I swallowed hard and stepped into Garrett's hospital room. The sight of my five-year-old was a shock. The blood from the wounds on his face had already turned a crusty black. At first glance, it looked like all of his teeth had been knocked out from the impact.

"Hi, Garrett." I forced a smile and leaned down to kiss his forehead. "Where did you get this stuffed bear? He sure is cute."

"From the ambulance man," Garrett said with gleaming eyes.

Like many young boys, Garrett was fascinated by emergency professionals. His favorite TV program was *Rescue 911*. Before the show would start, he'd line up all of his electronic emergency vehicles on the carpet in front of the TV. His collection of fire trucks, police cars, and ambulances were ready for action. I never imagined he would be a victim in his own episode.

"We need to check for internal injuries," said Dr. Mantor. "Since Garrett can't swallow the contrast dye, I'll need to insert a tube up his nose and down his throat to inject the dye for the x-ray. Would you like to stay in the room and hold his hand?"

"Of course." I gulped, fighting back tears. Never mind that I couldn't even watch my own blood being drawn.

The rest of the day was a blur. Between all the phone calls and the multitude of visitors, I barely remember a thing, except that an odd but welcome sense of peace began to settle on me.

I wasn't sure if I was numb to the tragedy or preoccupied with the whirlwind of visitors who came to share their condolences. I could only hope the peace would last. But I had no idea how I'd tell Garrett that his little brother didn't survive.

Later that afternoon, the x-rays came back, and Dr. Mantor delivered the only good news I would hear that day—Garrett had no internal injuries. He would stay at Children's Hospital to recover from the hairline fracture to his jaw, but he would make a full recovery.

After the visitors left, my body collapsed on the foldout chair that converted to a bed in Garrett's room. Exhausted, I somehow managed to drift off to sleep.

The next morning, just before I woke, the events of the previous day began to come into focus. Afraid to open my eyes and face the harsh reality, I resisted the urge to wake as long as possible. But I couldn't control my thoughts. They were there.

I remembered.

I remembered that Jake was gone.

I hadn't even seen his body yet. The coroner had to complete an autopsy. It was horrible that I couldn't see my baby. *Was he really dead?* I wondered if maybe they had made a mistake. The fact that I hadn't seen him yet teased my reasoning. My mind began to fill with other thoughts of what had happened the day before. I remembered that Garrett was injured. I remembered that my life had been shattered. I didn't want to remember. I wanted to escape. I wished my memory had channels like a TV. If I didn't like the program, I could just change the station and pretend like nothing ever happened.

I expected to wake up in utter despair, but instead, as I opened my eyes, I became aware of a presence—a powerful presence. A calmness and serenity. An overwhelming peace.

And then, like a smoke machine fills a room with fog, a cloud of joy hovered over me until it consumed every inch of Garrett's hospital room. A joy so undeniable I felt paralyzed by its presence.

And then I felt His voice.

"Christy, I was there," I sensed the Lord whisper. "I was there at the accident. When the cars collided, my hand extended out of heaven to Jake. He whirled around to wave good-bye, exclaiming, 'See you later, guys! I'm out of here!'"

A smile caught a tear trickling down my cheek.

"I gave you the name Sierra long ago," God whispered, "to prepare you for the day I would change his name."

Change his name?

"I knew the plans I had for Jacob before he was born. He was a forerunner. But yesterday, true to his name, he got ahead by an unfair advantage. He preceded you into heaven. So today, I've given Jacob a new name because his character has changed. Today Jacob, the forerunner, has become Sierra, and now, he is in the presence of God."

My body froze at the revelation I'd tried to understand for the past three years. *That's why God whispered Sierra to me while I was pregnant with him.*

"I couldn't explain why until now. You wouldn't have understood. My plans for Jacob wouldn't make sense until his destiny intersected with his future."

Destiny...intersect?

"Don't you know that your destiny doesn't end with death?"

I didn't understand.

"Your days on earth are numbered, but those that overcome live eternally. Those who are in Me live on. They've overcome death. And to those who overcome, I give a new name."

I knew in the Bible it wasn't uncommon to get a new name. God changed several names in the scriptures to signify a change in character. He changed Abram to Abraham. He changed Jacob to Israel, Saul to Paul, Simon to Peter. He even gave Jesus another name—Immanuel. In fact, all of us will get a new name when we go to heaven. I remembered that Revelation 12:11 talked how about those who overcome will get a white stone with a new name. But I still couldn't understand how our destiny could live beyond our death.

"Christy, look at those flowers."

I glanced at the flowers my friends brought the day before. Beautiful purple and lavender blooms cascaded over the top of the square glass vase.

"It's a kingdom principle that something has to die in order to produce life. Those flowers are dead, but they can still produce life through the seeds they leave behind. The joy I'm giving you today is like those flowers. Most people enjoy the presence of flowers for a few days, but when their beauty begins to fade, they let the life wilt away and die. But some, wanting the beauty to live on, take the seeds and plant them so the beauty and life reproduces."

I looked at the flowers again. They were beautiful that day, but I knew I'd throw them away soon enough. In fact, a few of the blooms were already wilting.

"Like those flowers, Jake has left a seed behind. His character and destiny live on in you. The joy I've given you today is not just for you, so don't let My presence fade away. It's important that you stay in My presence because joy cannot grow outside of My shelter. Take the joy I've given you today and share it with others."

I sat up on the vinyl hunter green chair-bed and glanced out the window. The sky seemed to glisten like diamonds. *Jake's out there somewhere,* I thought. And even though I'd never see him again on this side of heaven, the race of his life wasn't finished.

Jacob, my forerunner, passed on his baton to me.

PONDER AND PRACTICE

1. God whispers in so many different ways. Check the following ways you've heard Him speak to you or sensed His presence. Through:
   - ○ dreams
   - ○ visions
   - ○ the Bible
   - ○ sermons
   - ○ worship
   - ○ nature

- signs
- a visitation of an angel (Mary and Joseph both had one)
- miracles and wonders
- messages conveyed in books or movies
- physical exercise
- prophetic words
- confirmations
- journaling
- other

2. When God speaks, His words are often a mystery. A puzzle. You may not understand everything. Yet. That's why it's important to wait. When we wait before the Lord, there's an inner witness that senses His voice. His spirit testifies with our spirit (Romans 8:16). He guides us into all truth and tells us what is yet to come (John 16:13). How do you think God guides you into truth?
3. Why do you think God wants to tell you what is yet to come?
4. The gospel of Luke chapter 1 records the account of how the angel of the Lord told Mary she was going to have a baby. She was also promised that "He will be great and will be called the Son of the Most High". How long do you think she had to treasure this word in her heart?
5. It would have been impossible for Mary to comprehend God's entire plan. If the angel told her the whole story from the get go, she would have been consumed with sorrow. Knowing that her child was to be a sacrificial lamb, a baby

born to die for the sins of the world, would have been traumatic without the gradual unfolding of God's mystery and the benefit of God's kingdom perspective. She had to treasure the promise long beyond her pregnancy and Jesus' birth and even past Jesus' death on the cross. The word from the angel was for a lifetime.

6. The same is true for you. God gives a glimpse of His plan for your future. If you don't understand it all, it's probably because He has only revealed it in part. Jesus said in John 16:12, "I have much more to say to you, more than you can now bear." What word from the Lord do you need to hide in your heart, to ponder and treasure?

HIS TRUTH

Isaiah 46:10 says this: "I make known the end from the beginning, from ancient times, what is still to come. I say, 'My purpose will stand, and I will do all that I please.'"

I love this promise! Like a captivating screenwriter who sprinkles hints of what is yet to come, God foreshadows our future. He makes known the end from the beginning. If you're careful to listen and wait, God prepares you by giving you His word in advance for a reason. His divine whispers often don't make sense until the veil is lifted. But one thing is certain—His word to you is your promised treasure. Ponder it. Wait for it. It will fuel your ability to endure and give you strength to fight and persevere. What you've treasured and preserved in your heart grows more precious as it ages. Don't stop believing. Stand guard at your watchtower. His word will come to pass.

- 17 -

SAFE IN THE KEEP

HURRICANE KATRINA WAS ONE of the most devastating tragedies in American history. When Katrina hit the city of New Orleans in August of 2005, I was working for a contractor for HUD in Oklahoma City. One day, our quiet office housed a team of twelve employees. The next week, our staff grew to over three hundred. Our job: assist affected homeowners with mortgage issues and renters with relocation efforts.

Our office handled thousands of calls per day. Desperate to find out if their husband, sister, or cousin made it out alive, evacuees cried on the phone for help. Some were inconsolable about pets they'd left behind. Contact with the outside world was limited since their cell phones had died and their laptops had floated away. Their daily task was to wait. Sitting for days in crowded makeshift shelters miles from home, they waited and waited for everything, including the simple opportunity to use the phone. Our phone lines didn't quit ringing for months.

Most evacuees had no way to travel. Their vehicles were back in the flooded streets, where eighty percent of the city was completely submerged. Many of the people were sick and needed medication, but their prescriptions had been destroyed. Calling the doctor for a refill was not an option, since the files in their doctors' offices were under water. Not all records were online, and valuable medical histories were lost.

I spoke with countless victims devastated by the monumental task of rebuilding or relocating. I listened to story after story of horrid details—people who lost family members and friends. People who lost every piece of furniture, every article of clothing, every picture ever taken, every legal document ever filed away.

Very few had jobs they could return to, so paychecks quit coming and money ran out. Devastation set like concrete. It took weeks before any federal assistance was available. Some received none.

At times, I would just wipe my eyes and say, "I'm so sorry." That was it. What else could I say? They knew I wasn't suffering. They knew I was in a dry office building somewhere in Oklahoma City. I still had my home, my job, my family. Bottom line: My life was quasi normal. Theirs was destroyed.

Even though we were there to help, some callers were demanding, rude, and belligerent. Some were impatient and hysterical. Some were suicidal. With all the overtime required, it was hard to stay positive and encouraging. But just when I thought I'd heard it all, I got a call from Brenda.

Brenda had a different kind of attitude. She realized that what had happened was over and done with. While it changed her entire future, she was incapable of revising the tragedy. There was no delete button to press, no rewind to push. Plain and simple—she couldn't edit the past. The only thing she could change was her attitude. All she had control over now was her perspective. She'd lost her home, her neighborhood, her job, and her familiar surroundings. She had been involuntarily transplanted, but she decided to thrive, not just survive. She may have lost all her worldly possessions, but she didn't lose her faith.

Brenda had stored trust and confidence in her spiritual pantry for a rainy day. And what a rainy day it was—no pun intended. She chose to keep her focus ahead and remind herself that God is a God of restoration. I don't know what scriptures she had memorized or what church she went to. Our conversation wasn't that long. But whatever remnants of faith she'd stashed away now rose to the surface in her time of need. This is what she said to me.

"The hardest part is seeing the elderly suffer. The younger have longer to recover, but many of the elderly have no other resources. Still, I know that recovery lies ahead. I believe that if we were the ones chosen to endure this hardship, then God will give us the grace to endure. The destruction of our city has given birth to a spirit of unity."

I marveled at Brenda's choice—the choice to keep her focus beyond the storm.

"My hope isn't based on my circumstances," she continued. "If it was, I would be hopeless. I'm still in temporary housing miles from home. I haven't seen my house yet. I've heard that it's still underwater. At this point, I have no idea if rebuilding is even possible. But my hope is based on my decision to hope. Hope is a choice."

Brenda endured the same tragedy as hundreds of thousands of others, but she choose to leave the past behind. She couldn't change it. Instead she determined to look ahead and dwell on the future. She resolved to make the best of horrible circumstances. Brenda knew that focusing on past regrets would lead to depression. Focusing on future responsibilities would bring anxiety, but focusing on today would bring her peace.

Her focus kept her safe. Safe from the devastating circumstances because she refused to allow the storm to have control over her emotions. Brenda knew how to dwell in the shelter of the Most High. She knew how to stay in the castle keep.

THE CASTLE KEEP

The castle keep is a castle within a castle. It's a fortified high tower complete with living quarters used as a place of refuge should the rest of the castle fall under attack. In other words, a keep is a stronghold.

In the New Testament, the word *stronghold* comes from a Hebrew word that means a high place, a refuge, a secure height, a retreat, a high tower, or a high fort. David referred to the Lord as a strong tower (Psalm 61:3). He also called the Lord a "refuge for the oppressed, a stronghold in times of trouble" (Psalm 9:9).

That's what a castle keep is—a place where occupants are safe. By using this illustration in the Bible, David shows us a picture of how the Lord surrounds us with His protection. The battle may rage all around, but we're kept safe. The storm can't touch us when we stay in the keep.

I also compare the castle keep to the eye of a hurricane. As crazy as it seems, the center of the storm, the eye of a hurricane, is the safest place in a storm. The tempest is raging all around, but there's a place in the middle where the storm is calm. In fact, the eye is so safe that weather service planes fly into the eye of the storm to determine its ferocity.[21]

Likewise, there's a place in your storm where God keeps you safe. You have a stronghold, a castle keep that you can run to in times of trouble. When the enemy surrounds you, God surrounds you more. He offers his grace and protection in every storm. The choice to take it, however, is yours.

If we don't take the grace, we make ourselves vulnerable to bitterness. Listen to what Hebrews 12:15 says. I know I've mentioned this verse earlier, but I want to point out a few things by comparing three different versions.

The NIV: "See to it that no one *falls short* of the grace of God and that no bitter root grows up to cause trouble and defile many."

I have an older version of the NIV. (Yes, even translations are occasionally revised.) The 1991 version of the NIV says, "See to it that no one *misses* the grace."

But here's what I want you to see. The Phillips translation packs a powerful punch with its perspective. It says, "See to it that no one *fails to respond* to the grace of God."

Failing to respond to His grace would be like having the winning lottery ticket but never redeeming it. Or your friend calls to offer you a week at her timeshare in Hawaii, but you never listen to her voicemail and she gives it to someone else instead. You failed to respond.

Don't fall short of His grace. Don't miss it and fail to respond. You can't overcome without it. Hebrews makes it clear. When we fail to respond, we are putting ourselves in a place where bitterness can flourish.

God offered His grace to the hurricane survivors. Sadly, not everyone caught up in the hurricane aftermath took it. Some refused help. Thousands of residents ignored the call to evacuate and refused to leave even days after the storm subsided. Rescue boats and search crews combed the area, but the stubborn stayed. They stayed trapped inside the second stories of their flooded homes or in apartments or on roofs. They had no food or electricity. They had no jobs to go to and no phone service to contact loved ones. Yet, they didn't budge. Even with the risk of contracting a life-threatening gastrointestinal disease spreading through the polluted water, people turned down numerous offers to find safety.[22]

Many died in the city after the storm was over. They refused the offer to receive help and died in the very place they tried in their own strength to save. They denied the grace extended to them.

They failed to respond.

Whether the storm you face is a hurricane or an offense that develops into an emotional tsunami, God always offers his grace to endure or escape. Satan, on the other hand, wants to convince you that you're trapped—that you're chained to bitterness, sorrow, and depression. God has provided freedom, but blinders cause you to stay in bondage.

When the darkness of offense surrounds you, don't fret. It hurts, no doubt. But Jesus said offenses are impossible to avoid (Luke 17:1). Every offense is an opportunity to gain strength, but the pressure always comes before the promise. We even see this in nature. When an eagle pushes its eaglet out of the nest, the fall, which threatens to take its life, actually saves it. It's the push and the fall that make the eaglet fly.

Bishop T.D. Jakes said this about his book *Crushing: God Turns Pressure into Power* in an interview with Pastor Steven Furtick. "In the process of the eaglet falling, flapping its wings in hysteria, it is the thing that crushed the eaglet that causes it to soar… Crushing precedes a soaring. Crushing is the process. Soaring is the promise. You can't have a promise without process."[23]

In tragedy. In rejection, divorce, abuse, and abandonment—in every offense—God makes provision through His grace. He releases his power. Dear sister, when you feel like you're falling, flap your wings and take the grace. You're about to soar!

GRACE IS LIKE MANNA

Have you ever seen others walking through tragedies or difficulties with the undeniable power of God and thought to yourself, *There's no way I could do that* or *I hope that never happens to me. They have strength I don't have.* I've had thoughts like that, but here's the thing. If you're not in their shoes, you *don't* have the strength to face what they're facing. Until you are faced with the same issue, you *can't* handle it. Because God doesn't give His grace early.

God equips you with His grace and strength *when* you need it, not beforehand. Grace is a lot like the manna God gave the Israelites to feed them in the desert. Manna was a supernatural provision of bread God provided every morning to feed the people, but they still had to go out and gather it. Some gathered much and some gathered little, but when it was measured, he who gathered much did not have too much, and he who gathered little did not have too little. Each one had as much as he needed (Exodus 16:18). That's how His grace works, too. No matter how much you get, it's always exactly the right amount. It's never too much, and it's never too little.

But check this out. Manna can spoil. When the Israelites gathered too much and tried to save the leftovers for the next day, in the morning it was full of maggots and began to smell. Hmm… I think God is saying something here. He wants us to depend on

Him daily. He doesn't want us to hoard what we need. In order to be good, manna has to be fresh. Likewise, in order to be effective, grace has to be fresh.

We don't always need the same amount of grace each day. Some days are a breeze and some days are a bomb, but God meets our needs each day with just the right amount. His grace for each of us is based on our situation on an as-needed basis. He measures our needs and then supplies them. When we need more grace, He pours it out accordingly. No matter how big or small our situation is, His grace is always sufficient for our own areas of need (2 Corinthians 12:9).

I'm thankful that His mercies are new every morning. So the next time you're afraid of what the future holds, remember, God's grace rains down from heaven every morning. All you have to do is take it. I'm so glad I did. When Jake died and my own storm threatened to consume me, God poured out His grace and kept me safe in the keep. His protection has sustained me for over twenty years now. In my mind's eye, Jake is still a toddler, but I know in God's eyes he is a mighty warrior.

PLANNING JAKE'S FUNERAL

The lobby in the funeral home boasted Italian marble floors, rich mahogany furnishings, and chandeliers dripping with crystals. Exquisite artwork embellished three walls, and a mirror the size of Rhode Island adorned the other. It was a beautiful place, and yet so sterile and cold. I sat alone. Waiting. With nowhere else to look, I caught a glance of my reflection. My cheeks were vibrating. Although my feet were neatly crossed under the table in the waiting

Every offense is an opportunity to gain **strength,** but the pressure always comes before the **promise.**

room, my right foot trembled.

I never could sit still. I remember attending mass as a young girl. My father had the unique ability to both whisper and shout at the same time.

"Chrissie! *Sit still*," he scolded at least a thousand times.

I tried then and I tried that day. I still can't sit still.

Finally, the door opened. "Christy," said the funeral director, "my name is Michael. Right this way, please."

Michael opened the door to another room, offered his condolences, and opened a portfolio. "Which style of program do you have in mind for Jake's memorial service?"

I glanced at the choices. One picture showed eagles flying above mountains. Another depicted flowers blooming by quiet streams. They both seemed suitable for someone much older. Jake was two.

"Do you have anything for toddlers?" I asked.

Michael shook his head in slow motion.

I let out a sigh. "Let me see what I can create."

Next Michael slid some paperwork across the table. "I'll need you to complete this."

I glanced at the insurance portion. A few weeks earlier, I'd received a form at work in my benefits update package at the bank I worked for. It included life insurance for my dependents. I never thought I'd need to use it.

"I have the information at my office, but I haven't been back to work since the accident."

"Let me give the HR department at your bank a call," said Michael. "I'll be right back."

After several minutes passed, I started to wonder what was taking so long. My fingers tingled as I stroked the nubby fabric of the chair I was sitting in. Finally, the door opened again. Something in the director's stance communicated bad news.

"I'm sorry," Michael began. "Human Resources never received your completed insurance forms. You'll have to make other arrangements for the funeral expenses."

What?

My heart felt like hot liquid. How was I going to take care of expenses of this magnitude? Not knowing what else to do, I assured Michael that I would take care of it somehow. I managed to maintain my composure, but once in the privacy of my vehicle, I collapsed in tears. Pounding the steering wheel of my red Taurus, I screamed. "God, You're going to have to help me! I can't do this!"

From somewhere inside, my mind whispered the thought, "Be still and know that I am God."

"Now is not the time to sit still!" I shouted, arguing with myself and the empty air. "Funerals can't wait. I need the money now!"

When I got home, I threw my keys on the kitchen counter and stared out the window for a moment in disbelief. I grabbed a cookie and hit the play button on my answering machine.

"Christy, this is Debbie in Human Resources."

Yes, I know... No coverage.

"We are so sorry for your loss. The bank president heard about Jake's accident and immediately advised me to have the bank take care of the funeral."

I sank on a counter barstool sobbing as a wave of gratitude melted over me. Everything from Jake's plot, grave marker, custom programs, and a memorial video were covered in full. I had no insurance coverage, but God was faithful. He covered me instead.

AN ESCORT TO HEAVEN

As thankful as I was, I still worried about Garrett and how I was going to tell him about Jake. How do you tell a five-year-old that his best friend, his roommate, and the little brother he'd always protected was no longer there? How do you explain death to a child? I'd decided to wait until he asked about Jake. But now it was three days after the accident, and he still hadn't asked about him—or his dad, for that matter.

With the funeral fast approaching, my fiancé John was concerned. "Do you want me to talk to him?"

"No." I sighed. "I have to do this myself."

Garrett's face brightened as I entered his room. "Look, Mommy! Bruce from my daycare brought me some more stuffed animals. *And the Transformer I wanted*—Optimus Prime."

"That's nice, honey." I scooted a chair beside his bed.

"Garrett," I began.

"Yeah, Mommy?"

The room was warm, but I felt frozen.

"What would you say if I told you…" I stalled, gasping for air.

Garrett arranged a stuffed animal on his bed.

"It's Jake," I said. "Jake…didn't…make it." Tears streamed down my face. I couldn't even look up.

"Mom, I already know."

He already knows? I sat up straight and leaned forward. "What do you mean?"

"After the accident, I got to go to heaven with Jake." Garrett smiled as he swooped Optimus Prime into the air. He made gun sounds as he beat up his invisible enemies, "Jake got to go in, but God told me it wasn't my time."

Suddenly, I was on the edge of my seat. "What was heaven like?"

"Mommy!" Garrett's eyes squinted with apparent irritation. He set his Transformer down. A bewildered look spread across his face. "Mommy! I can't tell you that!"

"Why not?" I insisted.

"It's a surprise!"

I could hardly believe what I was hearing. I took a big gulp of air. "I'm sure God won't mind if you tell me, Garrett." I scooted my chair closer to his bed and stroked his hair. "He'll understand, honey. I'm your *mother*."

"No, Mommy, I *can't!*"

"Why not?"

"Cuz!"

"Cuz why?"

"Cuz God told me it's a secret."

Garrett went back to playing with his toys while I sat back in my chair, flabbergasted. Awed. *Garrett sure picked a good time to start keeping secrets.* In the past, he'd flunked confidentiality, but now his lips were locked.

Garrett's peace magnified my own. We both spoke at Jake's funeral. I held the microphone while he shared his story about escorting his little brother to heaven in front of hundreds of attendees. In the days and weeks following his release from the hospital, I tried to squeeze details out of Garrett, but he never uttered a single clue. His childlike trust amazed me, yet I fought skepticism. Did Garrett really take a trip to heaven, or was his story a figment of his five-year-old imagination?

Preschoolers can make up some enchanting stories. If it was

make-believe, however, it worked for him. He didn't grieve like the grief-recovery books that well-meaning friends had given me predicted. He never had a nightmare about the accident. And even though his dad was driving under the influence of several narcotics and received a deferred sentence for negligent homicide, Garrett held no bitterness toward his dad. Even so, my curiosity was hard to hush. I couldn't understand why he wouldn't tell me more about his trip to heaven.

Until I found the reason for his peculiar silence.

One day, I was reading my morning devotional and came across a story in the Bible about a man who'd been to heaven. He couldn't describe what he saw because it was a secret. I was spellbound. In the book of 2 Corinthians, the Apostle Paul says that he was caught up in the third heaven where he heard inexpressible things—*things that man was not permitted to tell.*

Paul experienced the same kind of secret quest that Garrett had witnessed.

I lingered over the verses for a moment. *What Garrett saw, he wasn't permitted to tell. That's why Garrett couldn't disclose details about his heavenly encounter. It really was a secret. It wasn't a fairy tale…it was a faith tale.*

I closed my Bible. As the pages fluttered together, my doubts finally vanished. Who was I to contend with a divine mystery? Awestruck, I realized that his journey to heaven empowered him with peace in the midst of disaster. Never again will I doubt the faith of a child, nor God's ability to provide peace in the midst of tragedy.

Especially to his precious little children.

OWN THE OUTCOME

My dear sister, if you focus on your offenses, you'll never witness the glory of the outcome. Don't deny His strength. His grace keeps pace with whatever you face, but in order for you to experience it, you have to take it. You can't live without it. Oh, you can endure, but that's not really living. Why would you want to face difficulties, betrayal, divorce, rejection, abuse, or adultery all by yourself when you can overcome in the midst of them with God's grace?

The Apostle Paul said that he delights in weaknesses, in insults, in hardships, in persecution and difficulties because when he is weak, then he is strong. Honestly, his statement in 2 Corinthians 12:10 is a hard pill to swallow. It's easier to see how God brings good after our crisis is over. But it is possible for us to see our situation from God's perspective before the issue resolves. In the middle of our circumstance, if we accept God's grace, we have a tremendous advantage. We can have peace, confidence and joy in the middle of chaos, not just when the crisis ends.

People tell me all the time how strong I am, but what they fail to realize is that it's not my strength. When God extends His grace, it's borrowed strength. It's strength delivered when we take the grace and stay in the keep.

Smith Wigglesworth says this about the power of Christ dwelling in us: "It can transform you so that you can be in Jesus Christ and know that it is another power dominating, controlling, filling you, and making you understand that though you are still in the body, you are governed by the Spirit."[24]

I want to encourage you to be governed by the Spirit. Stay in the safe place. The castle keep is your stronghold. When storms rage around you, He's got you covered. Even in sorrow. Even in hardship. Even in a hurricane.

PONDER AND PRACTICE

Author Alex Elle says this about difficulties: "I'm thankful for my struggle because without it I wouldn't have stumbled across my strength."

1. In retrospect, what strengths have your difficulties and offenses developed in you?
2. How can this hindsight encourage you next time you experience an offense?
3. Write out a prayer giving God thanks for how He's strengthened you.

- 18 -

Free at Last

AS SOON AS BRITTANY OPENED the door to her grandparents' two-bedroom home, I saw Tom in his usual spot—asleep on the recliner. My eyes narrowed, and my jaw clenched. Two years had passed since the accident, and it was beyond me that his folks allowed him to live there for so long without insisting that he find a job. But they continued to enable him. Even though his addiction to opioids had ruined our marriage and stolen my son, they took his side. In their eyes, the divorce had been my fault and the accident had nothing to do with Tom's drug use.

After the accident, Tom spent a couple of weeks in the hospital recovering from his physical injuries. Even though he was heavily medicated and could barely walk, he demanded that his doctor release him to attend Jake's funeral service. He arrived in his hospital gown using a walker and an IV pole for support.

While planning the funeral, I told my pastor, Boe Parrish, that I wanted to speak at Jake's service. He tried to talk me out of it, thinking that my emotions would get the best of me. But I refused. I couldn't contain myself. The joy God gave me after Jake died was profound, and I wanted everyone to hear about it. Before I left the stage, I locked eyes with Tom from the pulpit and forgave him right there in front of everyone. Grief stricken as any mother would be, the years of practice I'd had in forgiving him for everything under the sun had changed me. I knew if I held on to my offense, I'd go straight back to the bondage of bitterness I'd once lived in.

Still, I struggled. Even though I'd forgiven him, remarried a wonderful man, and moved on with my life, I didn't understand why I couldn't stop being so disgusted by him. Often I wondered, *Why is he still here? Why didn't God take him? Why did God allow him to survive and my innocent baby to die?*

When Tom was released from the hospital, he was transferred to a psychiatric facility in Norman, where he spent several weeks. When he returned home to his parent's house, I vowed he'd never drive my children anywhere again, and thankfully the court agreed with me on that point. In other matters, they disagreed. He only received a deferred sentence for Jake's death and served no jail time. In addition, the judge denied my petition to have Tom's parental rights dismissed and forced me to maintain Brittany and Garrett's weekend visitations every other week at his parents' home, where he still lived.

Tom's father typically picked up the kids on Friday at my house, and I'd drive to Del City to take them back home on Sundays. It was so unfair. Tom barely paid any attention to them. As much as he claimed to love his children, even years after the accident, he was so consumed with his own sorrow, he couldn't function. Frequent trips to the psych ward became his new normal. But as soon as he was out, he'd demand to see his kids. "If you don't let me have my children, I'll take you back to court!"

Here I was, two years after Jake's death, picking up the children after one of their weekend visits. Garrett jumped up to give me a hug. His hair smelled like an ashtray. I forced a smile. "How was Toy Story 2?"

"We didn't go yet. Daddy didn't have the money, but he promised to take us next time."

Brittany squeezed her arms around my waist.

"How long has your dad been asleep?" I demanded.

"Mom, it's okay. Don't worry. Dad said he doesn't feel well. He's only been asleep a few hours."

I stepped around the scattered pillows, dirty clothes, and a couple of their cousin's baby bottles half-filled with milk on the floor. Tom opened his glassy eyes in slow motion. "Hi, honey. You here to pick the kids up already?"

I crossed my arms and felt my stomach tighten. *How dare he still call me honey!*

"Garrett's teeth haven't been brushed all weekend," I said. "And you promised to take them to a movie, but *that* didn't happen! Can you not even spend one decent weekend with your children?"

I picked up Garrett's pajamas off the fold-out couch and put them in his backpack. "Come on, kids, it's time to go."

I opened the car door, and Garrett climbed into the backseat. "Mommy, why are you always so mad at Daddy?"

"Because he's obviously using drugs again."

Garrett's bottom lip quivered. "Mommy, Daddy says that's not true. He doesn't do drugs!"

It angered me that Garrett believed his dad. I wanted him to know the truth. I didn't want him to be deceived by Tom's manipulation and learn to ignore danger.

Hadn't Jake's death been proof enough? I wasn't making this drug thing up. Toxicology reports proved that he was driving under the influence of a cocktail of narcotics. But nothing I said convinced Garrett otherwise. To him, his dad could do no wrong.

I felt it was my duty to show my kids what to look for so that they could protect themselves. My motives backfired. Although in time, Brittany grew disinterested in going to her Dad's, Garrett adored his father. When he started talking about the day he'd go live with him, I didn't know what to do. As long as I could help it, there was no way that'd ever happen.

I once heard a saying that children learn what they live. I didn't want Brittany and Garrett to wallow in bitterness like I once had. As they grew older, I did my best to hide my feelings of disgust toward Tom for their benefit, but every time I saw him, they rose back to the surface again. By now he was behind on child support to the tune of $60,000. His slurred speech, weight gain, and filthy clothes were evidence that his addiction was growing. *Why couldn't he try to get better. At least for his kids? He knew the Lord. Why couldn't he conquer this addiction?*

Tom's parents both passed away in 2008. After they died, Tom moved in with his brother Carl and his wife. At that point, Brittany was twenty-two and Garrett was sixteen. Weekend visitations stopped with Garrett's busy high school schedule.

Around this time, I heard a message my pastor preached about honoring our parents. He quoted Ephesians 6:2-3, which reads, "'Honor your father and mother'—which is the first commandment with a promise—'so that it may go well with you and that you may enjoy long life on the earth.'"

The pew felt frozen: *Had I taught my children to dishonor their father?* I didn't want them to miss out on their blessing, but I had no clue how to teach them to honor a father they couldn't respect.

My pastor brought clarity to my quandary. I'd always thought honor and respect were the same, but he taught that they were different. Honor is due to the position, but respect is given by the person. Honor is required, but respect is earned. In other words, we can still give honor to someone we don't respect. That's why when David was pursued by King Saul, David said, "Far be it from me to lay a hand on the king." He gave honor to a king who tried to kill him, but that didn't mean he respected his character. Nor did he put himself in harm's way. When Saul sought to kill David, David retreated. Yet David still refused to kill Saul even when he had the chance.

Honor was required. Respect was not.

With this new insight, God was calling me to higher ground. John and I started inviting Tom to our house for the holidays. At least in the safety of our home, he could spend time with Brittany and Garrett, and we could keep an eye on him.

Tom was elated.

I couldn't wait until he left.

By then, I'd graduated past the loathing stage to a place where I loved him "in the name of the Lord." But my smug sentiment was just self-righteous pride. Two hours was about the maximum amount of time I could tolerate his presence.

That all changed one summer morning in 2012. I was waking up, and, as I barely opened my eyes, I had a vision of Tom running down the hallway toward my bedroom. He was young and healthy, clean and sober. And he'd lost the two hundred pounds he'd gained. As he approached my doorway, he didn't stop running. Like a best friend exploding with joy to share some wonderful news, he threw his arms into the air and dived onto my bed as if it were a swimming pool. A smile bigger than Mount Zion spread across his face. I never heard the news he wanted to share, but as the sun streamed through the white linen sheers in my bedroom, I sensed God whisper. *Christy, that's how I see Tom. He is my child. I don't see him bound by addiction. I see him redeemed, restored, and whole.*

In that moment, my hatred melted and hope flooded my heart. When Tom came over for Thanksgiving dinner that year, I invited him in with a smile and a warm embrace. "So glad you could make it."

Tom beamed. Brittany and Garrett shrugged their shoulders and exchanged confused glances. I no longer had to pretend or manufacture compassion for him. I saw past his pain. I saw Tom, not his brokenness.

Instead of the recovery I'd expected to see, however, his addiction to pain meds grew worse. His brother Carl had recently received a sizable insurance death benefit after his twenty-one-year-old son died of an overdose. Brittany told me Carl spent most of it on Oxycontin. In 2014, Carl was driving. He and Tom were on their way to a methadone clinic when Carl plowed into a truck. The other driver died at the scene, and Carl died later that day.

This was the second fatality accident Tom was involved in. None of his family wanted to deliver the news. "You should do it, Christy," his sister said. When he woke up two days later, John and I went to see him in the ICU. I took Tom's hand in mine. "Carl's in heaven now, but you're alive for a reason. You'll make it out of this." I prayed hard that Tom wouldn't spiral into despair.

Tom spent four months in the hospital recovering. He healed from his physical injuries but gave up on life. His brother was dead. His parents were gone, and he was at odds with his sister, his only other sibling. Living on his disability check left him few options. He begged Garrett to let him live with him, but Garrett knew better now. Since he had nowhere to go, Brittany helped him find an apartment.

Over the next several years I had long phone conversations with Tom. I was his only friend. Several times I reminded him about the vision I'd had. "God's not finished with you yet, Tom. You've survived two fatality accidents. He still has a purpose and a plan for you."

In 2017, when Tom's health declined and he was no longer capable of caring for himself, Brittany moved him into a nursing home. Even so, my hope remained. I couldn't erase the vision.

A day after my birthday in October of 2018, Brittany and I planned an afternoon of looking at houses together.

"Mom, before we leave, I've got something to tell you." She put her purse down on the white granite countertop in my kitchen and waited for my attention.

I finished putting on my jacket. "What is it, dear?"

Her eyes scrunched tight, and she hung her head. "I didn't want to tell you yesterday. And ruin your birthday."

"But?"

"Tom passed away yesterday."

"No!" I collapsed in a heap on the breakfast table and buried my face in my hands. Sobbing heaves spewed like a geyser.

Brittany wrapped her arms around me. She'd long lost respect for her father. That's why, as an adult, she'd started calling him Tom instead of Dad. "I didn't realize you'd take it so badly. I'm sorry, Mom."

"What happened?"

"I'm not sure. The nursing home called me last week and said they brought in Hospice."

"Did you go see him?"

"No, I didn't realize he'd go so quickly. I figured he'd have at least a few more months."

I wept knowing that Tom had died alone.

Disappointment washed over me as reality sunk in. I'd never see his restoration on this side of heaven. Later, I cried out to God, "Why did you give me that vision if it was never going to come to pass?"

A couple of days later, I sat down to read my Bible. Sometimes when I don't know what to read, I just open and start wherever my eyes land. I call it Bible Roulette. Such was the case this day. I opened to Habakkuk and started in chapter two, but I didn't get far. Verse three jumped off the page: "For the revelation awaits an appointed time; it speaks of the end and will not prove false. Though it linger, wait for it; it will certainly come and will not delay."

I closed my Bible. That one verse said it all. Even though the vision didn't happen the way I wanted…

Tom really was restored—not in life.

But in death.

And in the process, we both found freedom. He from his addiction. And I from the burden of my own hatred.

I thought of Tom running down the hallway and laughed out loud. Dying on my birthday was just like him. The man I finally learned to love crashed my party. With a smile bigger than Mount Zion, he came to let me know—he was free at last.

And so am I.

WEARING THE CROWN

Freedom is yours for the taking, too. God wants your castle filled with His delight, and, when you overcome, He has a crown of authority for you.

So, I think it's celebration time. If you've made it this far, your perseverance tells me that you're ready. Without your crown, your kingdom won't be complete. Every feature you've created in your castle has built a foundation for this final embellishment.

You've installed windows so you can see where the enemy has tried to gain access. You've installed a door so you can decide which thoughts you want to allow access. You've installed a moat, which protects your property with boundaries to keep the enemy out.

Your castle is lit with the presence of the Holy Spirit, and you've added buttresses so that your foundation is supported by God's truth. You even have a watchtower to see things from Gods perspective. And lastly, you've learned how to dwell in the shelter of the Most High and stay in the stronghold, the castle keep.

Building your castle has been hard work, but you've removed the victim badge and let God finish the work He began in you. You've gone from wreckage to reign, from broken to brave, from slave to sovereign, and from casualty to queen! Now the only thing your castle lacks is a crown. Are you ready to wear it?

Your crown was created out of tremendous suffering, but it comes with the sovereign power and protection of the King. Wearing it means you've endured and arrived victorious. It means you've allowed God to give His glory in exchange for your offenses. That's the beauty of the crown. Every jewel in your headpiece was handcrafted by the Master Jeweler to showcase His glory in you. I love that God doesn't waste our hurts. Instead, He creates purpose out of pain and joy out of sorrow.

Proverbs 19:11 says that it's to our glory to overlook an offense. It's interesting that the word *overlook* used in this verse is the same Hebrew word *abar* used to describe how the Lord passed over and protected the Hebrews from the destroyer. You probably remember the story of the ten plagues in the book of Exodus. The last plague—the death of all firstborn sons—is detailed in chapter 12. It was the final call to convince Pharaoh to let God's people go. God, however provided a way of escape for His children.

If the Hebrews covered their doorposts with the blood of a lamb, the Lord would *pass over* or *overlook* their doorway and not allow the destroyer to enter their house. Likewise, when you forgive, the enemy has no authority to enter your castle. When you overlook offenses, you put the enemy on lock-down. He's not able to enter your castle. Why? Because there's no longer an entry point. The Lord becomes your security guard. He fights your battles for you. God Himself keeps the destroyer away from your castle.

The enemy can't use his evil tactics to enslave you any longer. Despair, bitterness, sorrow, and grief—they no longer have power over you.

Freedom has come.

Freedom was birthed out of slavery, but it produced tremendous power and confidence. Strength came from betrayal. Beauty came from brokenness, and glory rose up out of the soil of suffering. These are all kingdom principals. Even the Messiah had to suffer these things and then enter his glory (Luke 24:26).

YOU ARE THE TROPHY CASE

The promise in Isaiah 61:3 highlights God's purpose. He never intended for you to stay stuck in your pain. God wants to bestow on you a crown of beauty instead of ashes, the oil of joy instead of mourning, and a garment of praise instead of a spirit of despair. He wants to call you an oak of righteousness, a planting of the LORD for the display of his splendor.

God longs to reveal His glory to the world, but He needs a human trophy case to display it in. And that is you, adorned with the jewels of your testimony. You wear His living proof that He is able.

Your crown is adorned with costly gems, even though they were created from despiteful things. Dirt. Coal. Suffering. Adversity. Offenses. Don't you find that interesting since we were made from dust? But that's God's specialty. He makes beautiful things out of nothing. All He has to do is breathe on something, and life comes forth. Beauty comes forth. Strength, power, and freedom come forth.

Think about natural jewels. Pearls and diamonds are created out of tremendous adversity and pressure. A pearl forms when an irritant, such as a grain of sand, works its way inside an oyster's shell. The oyster struggles to remove it, but can't. So, as a way of dealing with the irritation, the oyster secretes a fluid to coat the pain and nuisance. Layer upon layer of this coating is deposited on the offending intruder until a lustrous pearl is formed. The whole process takes several years. And it all started with a tiny grain of sand—an irritant of offense.

In a similar way, a diamond doesn't look pretty in its raw form. A diamond evolves from an ordinary lump of coal. Many of us

You are an oak of righteousness, a *planting* of the LORD for the display of his *splendor.*

wouldn't recognize a diamond if we saw it in pure form. We certainly wouldn't want to put one on our finger or around our neck. Before a diamond has a shiny sparkle, it looks more like a simple black rock. It's just a chunk of carbon. But when this undistinguished run-of-the-mill stone goes through the fire and gets polished, it radiates beauty.

After a jeweler cuts a diamond, the end result is a rock that weighs much less than it did at the start. According to Wikipedia, "the cutting and polishing of a diamond crystal always results in a dramatic loss of weight; rarely is it less than fifty percent."[25]

The same is true for you. When the Master Jeweler shapes you, He's attempting to get rid of excess flesh. He knows just what to extract that will produce the maximum clarity and shine. Then He must polish you so that His glory shines from every facet. It's not a pleasant experience when you're going through the heat of adversity, but when you come out on the other side, you'll reflect His glory.

The diamonds in your crown are also created from adversity. In their final form, however, they symbolize purity and strength. In fact, the word diamond comes from the Greek word *adamas*, which means "invincible."

Oh, the beauty. When you come out of the fire, you're radiant and glorious. You're admired, not for your own shine, but for the illumination of the light within—the light of Christ. I hope you'll say it was all worth it. No matter how much it hurt to endure the process, once the brilliancy of Christ shines in you, I pray you'll never look back or trade the life you have now for your former existence.

The words of the Apostle Paul in 2 Corinthians 4:17 say it best. "For this light and momentary affliction is preparing for us an eternal weight of glory beyond all comparison."

This scripture is a stunning reminder that brokenness and betrayal can produce magnificent beauty and incomparable strength. In God's kingdom, your suffering is not in vain. God needs you to showcase His glory.

So stand tall in your castle, sister. It's time to put on your crown and let the light of Christ shine in you!

ENDNOTES

[1] http://www.huffingtonpost.com/2013/07/02/cheating-wives_n_3536412.html. Accessed January 6, 2017.

[2] https://www.onenewsnow.com/culture/2014/10/09/survey-alarming-rate-of-christian-men-look-at-porn-commit-adultery. Accessed January 7, 2017.

[3] http://www.divorcestatistics.info/divorce-statistics-and-divorce-rate-in-the-usa.html. January 5, 2017.

[4] http://www.theboxofdaughter.com/Statistics_on_Emotional_Abuse.pdf. Accessed January 7, 2017.

[5] http://www.foxnews.com/healt+h/2011/11/17/one-in-five-american-adults-takes-psychiatric-drugs/. Accessed January 5, 2017.

[6] http://ncadv.org/files/National%20Statistics%20Domestic%20Violence%20NCADV.pdf. Accessed January 5, 2017.

[7] Black, M. C., Basile, K. C., Breiding, M. J., Smith, S .G., Walters, M. L., Merrick, M.T., … Stevens, M. R. (2011). *The National Intimate Partner and Sexual ViolenceSurvey: 2010 summary report.* Retrieved from the Centers for Disease Control and Prevention, National Center for Injury Prevention and Control: http://www.nsvrc.org/sites/default/files/publications_nsvrc_factsheet_media-packet_statistics-about-sexual-violence_0.pdf. Accessed January 7, 2017.

[8] http://www.rrsonline.org/?page_id=944. Accessed January 7, 2017.

[9] http://www.dailymail.co.uk/health/article-2024386/Harbouring-bitterness-increases-likelihood-physical-disease.html. Accessed January 8, 2017.

[10] https://www.justice.gov/ovw/domestic-violence. Accessed January 8, 2017.

[11] Robia Scott, *Counterfeit Comforts* (Ada, Michigan: Chosen Books: 2016), 19.

[12] Adapted from *Let's Get Real* by Manda Mandrell, pages 96-111.

[13] Alexander Loyd, PhD, ND, *The Healing Code* (New York: Grand Central Life & Style, 2010), 14.

[14] Oprah Winfrey, "What Oprah Knows for Sure About Trusting Her In-

tuition," http://www.oprah.com/spirit/oprah-on-trusting-her-intuition-oprahs-advice-on-trusting-your-gut#ixzz5iAzokPAf. Assessed January 13, 2020.

[15] https://www.boundariesbooks.com/boundaries/test-quality-relationship/?utm_source=hccp&utm_medium=email&utm_campaign=ZN-BO%20 20181119%20How%20to%20Test%20the%20Quality%20of%20Any%20 Relationship%20(1)&utm_content=. Accessed March 22, 2019.

[16] https://www.goodreads.com/work/quotes/56765588-finish-give-yourself-the-gift-of-done. Accessed March 25, 2019.

[17] https://acuff.me/2015/01/learning-tell-someone-no/. Accessed March 21, 2019.

[18] ODAT, January 2. http://alanonreadings.blogspot.com/. Accessed April 18, 2019.

[19] Leslie Vernick, The Emotionally Destructive Marriage: How to Find Your Voice and Reclaim Your Hope, WaterBrook Press, 2013, Chapter 7, pg 112-113.

[20] https://www.ted.com/talks/anne_lamott_12_truths_i_learned_from_life_and_writing. Accessed April 29, 2019.

[xxi] https://sciencing.com/definition-eye-wall-hurricane-6504125.html. Accessed April 11, 2019.

[21] https://www.latimes.com/archives/la-xpm-2005-sep-06-na-katrina6-story.html. Accessed April 16, 2019.

[22] https://www.youtube.com/watch?v=CzP23Zti-YI&feature=youtu.be, Accessed April 17, 2019.

[24] Smith Wigglesworth, *Smith Wigglesworth Devotional*, (Pennsylvania: Whitaker House, 1999) 174.

[25] https://en.wikipedia.org/wiki/Diamond_cut. Accessed April 17, 2019.

Connect with Christy

Christy Johnson
Soul Health Coach & Relationship Expert

freedom
in life, love & relationships

IS HE A FIT FOR YOU?

Get Christy's **free Dating Digest & Relationship Risk Assessment,** foolproof ways to know if he's right for you. Hop on over to www.isheafit.com to take the quiz.

Get the most out of *Free Looks Good on You* with the **companion curriculum or group coaching experience.** Get more details about **Let Go & Thrive** by visiting www.christyjohnson.org/let-go-and-thrive.

Find Christy's Bible plans on **YouVersion.**

Find out about Christy's coaching programs or invite her to speak at your next women's event.
Visit www.ChristyJohnson.org.
or contact Christy at Christy@ChristyJohnson.org.

www.ingramcontent.com/pod-product-compliance
Lightning Source LLC
Chambersburg PA
CBHW052013070526
44584CB00016B/1733